The Censorship Debate

T19725

Volume 121

Series Editor

Craig Donnellan

Assistant Editor

Lisa Firth

Independence

Educational Publishers
Cambridge

First published by Independence
PO Box 295
Cambridge CB1 3XP
England

British Library Cataloguing in Publication Data
The Censorship Debate – (Issues Series)
I. Donnellan, Craig II. Series
363.3'1

ISBN 1 86168 354 5

Printed in Great Britain
MWL Print Group Ltd

Layout by
Lisa Firth

Cover
The illustration on the front cover is by
Angelo Madrid.

CONTENTS

Chapter One: The Free Speech Debate

Chapter Two: Regulation and Censorship

Introduction

The Censorship Debate is the one hundred and twenty-first volume in the **Issues** series. The aim of this series is to offer up-to-date information about important issues in our world.

The Censorship Debate looks at the free speech debate, as well as the relationship between censorship and regulation.

The information comes from a wide variety of sources and includes:
Government reports and statistics
Newspaper reports and features
Magazine articles and surveys
Website material
Literature from lobby groups
and charitable organisations.

It is hoped that, as you read about the many aspects of the issues explored in this book, you will critically evaluate the information presented. It is important that you decide whether you are being presented with facts or opinions. Does the writer give a biased or an unbiased report? If an opinion is being expressed, do you agree with the writer?

The Censorship Debate offers a useful starting-point for those who need convenient access to information about the many issues involved. However, it is only a starting-point. Following each article is a URL to the relevant organisation's website, which you may wish to visit for further information.

*****

A free press

Who rules?

Can you imagine what life would be like without the media? No radio to listen to while you're getting ready for school, no Internet to trail through for information, no TV to watch for entertainment, no newspapers to read about the latest news from around the world. What would you do? Where would you get information from? What information would you need or want to hear and see? Why would you want it?

> *If some members of the press think the government is doing a bad job, then they should be free to say so. If others think the government is the best thing since sliced bread, then they too should be heard*

Media don't exist just to entertain us. In a democracy the media provide us with important information. They can give us a range of opinions which we might not otherwise hear.

No secrets

You probably agree that we should be free to access the information we're interested in. But is this always a good idea? What about during wartime? Do we need to know the ins and outs of the army's plans? If a newspaper printed where the army were planning on going and what they were going to do, could this cause problems? Information is generally free to come by unless it's very sensitive. In these cases it is censored.

Government control

Some countries don't have press freedom and their governments tightly control the media. They only want people to hear positive things about them so that they can stay in power. Furthermore, anyone who publishes or broadcasts something against the government faces stiff penalties – in some places this could even be death.

Censored

When there are restrictions on what people can see and hear, this is called censorship. By censoring something, you are preventing the whole truth coming out or stopping something being seen or heard at all. It's a bit like when you're watching something on TV and parts of the picture are blurred so you can't see, or when words are beeped.

Freedom of speech

That's what a free press is all about: allowing us to find out what we want to know without restrictions. If some members of the press think the government is doing a bad job, then they should be free to say so. If others think the government is the best thing since sliced bread, then they too should be heard.

Hearing different opinions allows us to make up our own minds instead of having them made up for us. An effective democracy is one where people know what's going on and so can make informed choices and decisions.

Secrets

Sometimes the government decides that some information is too sensitive to be out in the open and that it could place the country under threat (for example, information about terrorists, or military plans). Everyone who has access to this information,

such as government employees, has to sign the Official Secrets Act; if they reveal the information to anyone, they could be prosecuted and even imprisoned. Official Secrets must remain undisclosed for thirty years. After the time limit expires, the information is made available to the public.

Key points

- Democracies encourage a free press.
- A free press is allowed (within reason) to print and say what it likes about the government.
- Sometimes the government decides to restrict information during an emergency, such as a war.
- Being able to access different views and opinions allows us to decide what we think about issues for ourselves.

Some countries heavily censor and control the media in order to prevent any bad views about their government.

Reality bytes: the People's Republic of China and the Internet

The media in China are tightly controlled by the government. The government is particularly strict with the use of the Internet as it opens up access to all sorts of information. Everyone who wants to host their own website in China has to get a licence from the government. The content of the website also has to be approved. The government also controls what users can access on the Internet. Many websites are blocked by the government so that users are denied access.

The Freedom of Information Act states that there should be free access to information about the government, individuals and businesses

---

Getting information through

People in other countries try to find ways of letting Chinese Internet users access the forbidden sites by emailing instructions to individuals telling them how to bypass the rules, but the Chinese government employs people specifically to search for these emails and block them. Blocked websites include news sites from

other countries, sites that promote democracy and religious sites. There are penalties for people found to have broken the rules.

Interesting facts

- The Freedom of Information Act states that there should be free access to information about the government, individuals and businesses.
- 40% of homes in Britain have access to the Internet – that's around ten million people.

- The above information is reprinted with kind permission from Channel 4. For more information, please visit the Channel 4 website at www.channel4.com.

© *Channel 4*

Voting intention by newspaper readership

Voting intention	Daily Express	Daily Mail	The Mirror	Daily Telegraph	Financial Times	The Guardian	The Independent	Daily Star	The Sun	The Times
Conservative	44%	57%	13%	64%	36%	7%	11%	17%	35%	44%
Labour	29%	24%	66%	14%	34%	48%	38%	53%	44%	27%
Liberal Democrats	20%	14%	15%	18%	23%	34%	43%	13%	10%	24%
Scottish/Welsh Nationalist	2%	1%	1%	0%	1%	1%	0%	7%	5%	0%
Green Party	2%	1%	2%	1%	0%	7%	4%	3%	1%	2%
UK Independence Party	2%	2%	1%	2%	1%	0%	1%	3%	3%	2%
Other	2%	1%	1%	1%	5%	4%	3%	4%	2%	1%

MORI Voting Intention Aggregate (Certain to vote 10/10). Base: 11,786 GB adults aged 18+ (8,982 giving a voting intention), January-March 2005.

Source: MORI

Timeline: a history of free speech

By David Smith and Luc Torres

399BC Socrates speaks to jury at his trial: 'If you offered to let me off this time on condition I am not any longer to speak my mind... I should say to you, 'Men of Athens, I shall obey the Gods rather than you.'

1215 Magna Carta, wrung from the unwilling King John by his rebellious barons, is signed. It will later be regarded as the cornerstone of liberty in England.

1516 *The Education of a Christian Prince* by Erasmus. 'In a free state, tongues too should be free.'

1633 Galileo Galilei hauled before the Inquisition after claiming the sun does not revolve around the earth.

1644 'Areopagitica', a pamphlet by the poet John Milton, argues against restrictions of freedom of the press. 'He who destroys a good book, kills reason itself.'

1689 Bill of Rights grants 'freedom of speech in Parliament' after James II is overthrown and William and Mary installed as co-rulers.

1770 Voltaire writes in a letter: 'Monsieur l'abbé, I detest what you write, but I would give my life to make it possible for you to continue to write.'

1789 'The Declaration of the Rights of Man', a fundamental document of the French Revolution, provides for freedom of speech.

1791 The First Amendment of the US Bill of Rights guarantees five freedoms: of religion, speech, the press, the right to assemble and the right to petition the government for a redress of grievances.

1859 'On Liberty', an essay by the philosopher John Stuart Mill, argues for toleration and individuality. 'If any opinion is compelled to silence, that opinion may, for aught we can certainly know, be true. To deny this is to assume our own infallibility.'

1859 *On the Origin of Species*, by Charles Darwin, expounds the theory of natural selection. T.H. Huxley publicly defends Darwin against religious fundamentalists.

1929 Justice Oliver Wendell Holmes, of the US Supreme Court, outlines his belief in free speech: 'The principle of free thought is not free thought for those who agree with us but freedom for the thought we hate.'

1948 The Universal Declaration of Human Rights is adopted virtually unanimously by the UN General Assembly. It urges member nations to promote human, civil, economic and social rights, including freedom of expression and religion.

1770 – Voltaire writes: 'I detest what you write, but I would give my life to make it possible for you to continue to write'

1958 Two Concepts of Liberty, by Isaiah Berlin, identifies negative liberty as an absence or lack of impediments, obstacles or coercion, as distinct from positive liberty (self-mastery and the presence of conditions for freedom).

1960 After a trial at Old Bailey, Penguin wins the right to publish D H Lawrence's sexually explicit novel, Lady Chatterley's Lover.

1962 One Day In the Life of Ivan Denisovich by Aleksandr Solzhenitsyn describes life in a labour camp during Stalin's era. Solzhenitsyn is exiled in 1974.

1989 Iranian leader Ayatollah Khomeini issues a fatwa against Salman Rushdie over the 'blasphemous' content of his novel, The Satanic Verses. The fatwa is lifted in 1998.

1992 In Manufacturing Consent, Noam Chomsky points out: 'Goebbels was in favour of free speech for views he liked. So was Stalin. If you're in favour of free speech, then you're in favour of freedom of speech precisely for views you despise.'

2001 In the wake of 9/11, the Patriot Act gives the US government new powers to investigate individuals suspected of being a threat, raising fears for civil liberties.

2002 Nigerian journalist Isioma Daniel incenses Muslims by writing about the Prophet Muhammad and Miss World, provoking riots which leave more than 200 dead.

2004 Dutch film maker Theo van Gogh is killed after release of his movie about violence against women in Islamic societies.

2005 The Serious Organised Crime and Police Act bans protest without permit within 1km of the British Parliament.

5 February 2006

Freedom of expression

Information from the Foreign and Commonwealth Office

'Everyone has the right to freedom of opinion and expression; this right includes freedom to hold opinions without interference and to seek, receive and impart information and ideas through and media and regardless of frontiers.'
Article 19, Universal Declaration of Human Rights

Freedom of expression and opinion is a foundation without which many other basic human rights cannot be enjoyed. Allowing people to publicly investigate and report on human rights abuses makes it much harder for those responsible for them to hide behind a veil of silence and ignorance. Similarly freedom of expression makes a valuable contribution to other key areas of concern – good governance, rule of law and democracy. The media have a vital role in scrutinising and evaluating the actions of government, forcing them to manage resources and set policies in a transparent and equitable way. And without journalists having the right to report on court cases and legal judgements, it would be much harder to guarantee an independent and fair judicial process. Finally, the ability to hold, exchange and challenge the opinions of yourself and others is a necessary component of a functioning democracy.

Governments have a duty to eliminate barriers to freedom of expression and information, and to create an environment in which free speech and free media flourish. Media professionals should be able to work freely without fear of intimidation, violence or imprisonment. Sadly, there are still many countries around the world in which governments stifle dissent and criticism or fail to prevent other groups from targeting the media. A free and independent media requires governments to provide a fair and transparent regulatory environment, an equitable distribution of broadcasting frequencies and opportunities for all sections of society to access and contribute to the media.

■ The above information is reprinted with kind permission from the Foreign and Commonwealth Office. Visit www.fco.gov.uk for more information.

© Crown copyright

Media ownership and control

Who rules?

Would it matter if there was just one company that owned all the newspapers and all the TV channels? There would still be lots of different channels, some with sport, some with documentaries, some with films, and there'd be lots of newspapers too – tabloids and broadsheets. What do you think? What if the government owned all the newspapers and TV channels? There may still be lots of different channels and papers, but nevertheless you might think that the government was controlling what you read and saw.

Whose views?

What if the owner of a media company had strong beliefs about women – if they thought women should never be allowed to work, that they should stay at home, cook, clean and be mothers? Would that

---

The Sun is the biggest selling newspaper in the UK, followed by the Daily Mail. These two papers reach over six million people

---

bother you? Could it affect the types of films shown or what news we heard? What if the owner was racist and supported a political party with racist views? How might the owner's views affect what is being printed and broadcast?

Just as government control of the media can restrict the range of views and opinions expressed, so can the people who own and control the media companies.

Censorship or choice?
In the UK, a handful of companies own most of the media. The biggest company is the News Corporation. This company owns (among many others) *The Times*, *Sunday Times*, *The Sun*, *News of the World* and a large share of Sky Television. It provides a choice of news and entertainment, but many of the views and opinions expressed are quite similar, they are just presented in different ways.

Media companies tend to support one particular political viewpoint. This can have a huge influence on how people vote

---

Some people think this could be quite a problem, especially if the people that own the company have very specific political views. This could mean that just one point of view is being put across. So, even if the media aren't controlled by the government, one or two companies control most media instead. Do you think this should be allowed?

Reality bytes: the News Corporation
The News Corporation owns *The Times*, *Sunday Times*, *The Sun*, *News of the World* and part of Sky TV. Associated Newspapers owns the *Daily Mail*, *Mail on Sunday*, the *London Evening Standard* and has a share in ITN (Independent Television News). The Hollinger New Telegraph group owns the *Daily Telegraph* and the *Sunday Telegraph*.

All of these newspapers used to support the Conservative Party. At election time they would cover their pages with stories about how great the Tories were and how bad Labour were. For the 18 years that the Conservative Party was in power, the Party was supported by those newspapers. Labour had support from The Trinity Mirror Group (the *Mirror*, *Sunday Mirror* and *Sunday People*) and the Guardian Media Group (*Guardian* and *Observer*).

Then in 1997, The News Corporation changed to support Labour in the general election. Labour won. Do you think Labour's win was caused by this?

The big sellers
The Sun is the biggest selling newspaper in the UK, followed by the *Daily Mail*. These two papers reach over six million people. That doesn't include people who don't buy a copy. The third biggest selling paper is the *Mirror*, then the *Express* (also Conservative supporting), followed by the *Daily Telegraph* and *The Times*.

So, in the top six biggest selling newspapers, until 1997 there was just one (the *Mirror*) that supported the Labour Party. That means that most newspaper readers were getting Conservative points of view and opinions. How do you think that may have affected their voting at election time? The 18 years of the Conservatives being in power may help explain that!

Interesting facts
■ The BBC gets its money from the TV licence fee. Everyone who owns a TV has to have a licence.

In effect this means we own the BBC.
■ In 1936 a TV cost the same as a new car!

Big question
■ Britain currently has 11 national newspapers. Years ago there used to be many more. Do you think that the Internet will eventually mean newspapers will be extinct?

■ The above information is reprinted with kind permission from Channel 4. Visit www.channel4.com for more information.

© *Channel 4*

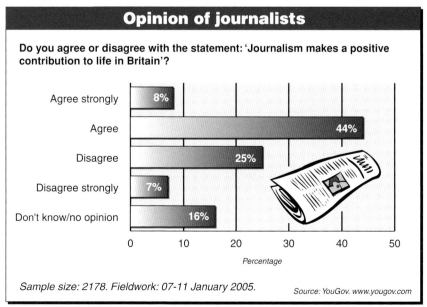

Opinion of journalists

Do you agree or disagree with the statement: 'Journalism makes a positive contribution to life in Britain'?

Agree strongly — 8%
Agree — 44%
Disagree — 25%
Disagree strongly — 7%
Don't know/no opinion — 16%

Percentage (0, 10, 20, 30, 40, 50)

Sample size: 2178. Fieldwork: 07-11 January 2005.

Source: YouGov. www.yougov.com

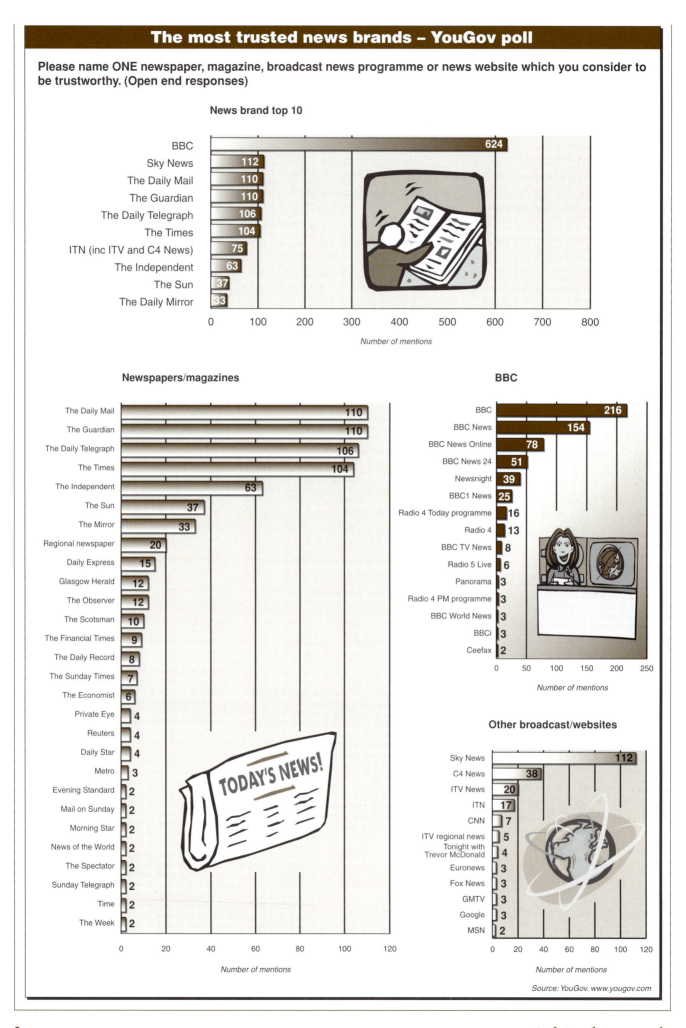

The most trusted news brands – YouGov poll

Please name ONE newspaper, magazine, broadcast news programme or news website which you consider to be trustworthy. (Open end responses)

News brand top 10

	Number of mentions
BBC	624
Sky News	112
The Daily Mail	110
The Guardian	110
The Daily Telegraph	106
The Times	104
ITN (inc ITV and C4 News)	75
The Independent	63
The Sun	37
The Daily Mirror	33

Number of mentions

Newspapers/magazines

	Number of mentions
The Daily Mail	110
The Guardian	110
The Daily Telegraph	106
The Times	104
The Independent	63
The Sun	37
The Mirror	33
Regional newspaper	20
Daily Express	15
Glasgow Herald	12
The Observer	12
The Scotsman	10
The Financial Times	9
The Daily Record	8
The Sunday Times	7
The Economist	6
Private Eye	4
Reuters	4
Daily Star	4
Metro	3
Evening Standard	2
Mail on Sunday	2
Morning Star	2
News of the World	2
The Spectator	2
Sunday Telegraph	2
Time	2
The Week	2

Number of mentions

BBC

	Number of mentions
BBC	216
BBC News	154
BBC News Online	78
BBC News 24	51
Newsnight	39
BBC1 News	25
Radio 4 Today programme	16
Radio 4	13
BBC TV News	8
Radio 5 Live	6
Panorama	3
Radio 4 PM programme	3
BBC World News	3
BBCi	3
Ceefax	2

Number of mentions

Other broadcast/websites

	Number of mentions
Sky News	112
C4 News	38
ITV News	20
ITN	17
CNN	7
ITV regional news	5
Tonight with Trevor McDonald	4
Euronews	3
Fox News	3
GMTV	3
Google	3
MSN	2

Number of mentions

Source: YouGov. www.yougov.com

UNESCO and World Press Freedom Day

Freedom of information and the press

UNESCO promotes freedom of expression and freedom of the press as a basic human right.

UNESCO, in keeping with its Constitution, advocates the basic human right of freedom of expression, enshrined in the Universal Declaration of Human Rights, and its corollary, press freedom. Indeed, since its creation in 1945, UNESCO has been called upon to 'promote the free flow of ideas by word and image', and the organisation's Member States have repeatedly confirmed this mandate over the years in decisions adopted by the General Conference, the highest authority of the United Nations agency. UNESCO promotes freedom of expression and freedom of the press as a basic human right.

Public's right of access to information

A free press is not a luxury that can wait for better times; rather, it is part of the very process which can bring about better times. Freedom of the press should not be viewed solely as the freedom of journalists to report and comment. It is strongly correlated with the public's right of access to knowledge and information. Communication often acts as a catalyst for the development of civil society and the full exercise of free expression enables all parts of society to exchange views and find solutions to social, economic and political problems. Free media play a crucial role in building consensus and sharing information, both essential to democratic decision-making and to social development.

In keeping with this mandate UNESCO has been working with professional organisations, and a wide range of governmental, as well as non-governmental partners, on several fronts to build up, support and defend free, independent and pluralistic media in developing countries, countries in transition and in conflict and post-conflict areas.

UNESCO's media work

UNESCO maintains close relations with regional and international media organisations and press freedom advocacy groups. One of its major partners is the electronic clearing-house and alert network, IFEX, which groups 500 member organisations in 130 countries. Since 1992, IFEX has facilitated the sharing of information about press freedom and the efficiency of reactions to cases of violations.

A free press is not a luxury that can wait for better times; rather, it is part of the very process which can bring about better times

---

Professional training for journalists

UNESCO recognises that media independence and freedom of information do not hinge only on the capacity of private individuals to operate media outlets; it also requires a commitment to professional standards of reporting. Thus UNESCO's work includes advocacy, professional training for journalists and media professionals, and support for professional networks, as well as providing governments with advice and information on best practices regarding media legislation and regulation.

World Press Freedom Day

Amidst the growing recognition of the importance of press freedom for democracy and development, in 1993 the United Nations General Assembly proclaimed that May 3 is 'World Press Freedom Day'. Throughout the world, this Day serves as an occasion to celebrate press freedom, raise awareness of violations against the right to freedom of expression and draw attention to the work of all too many journalists forced to brave death or jail to bring people their daily news. It is also on World Press Freedom Day that UNESCO awards the annual UNESCO/Guillermo Cano World Press Freedom Prize to a journalist who has distinguished him or herself in the fight for press freedom.

UNESCO is increasingly being asked to assist, together with the other United Nations system organisations, funds and programmes, in seeking solutions in conflict prevention, emergency assistance, and post-conflict peace-building. Freedom of the press, pluralism and independence of the media, and development of community newspapers and radio stations are crucial to the re-establishment of social bonds and to the reconciliation process.

■ The above information is reprinted with kind permission from the United Nations Educational, Scientific and Cultural Organization. Visit http://portal.unesco.org.

Grey area

The debate over academic freedom versus offensive views has become even more complex in light of David Irving's imprisonment and other recent events, writes Gargi Bhattacharyya

I've been worrying about what you should and should not be able to say.

The issue of causing offence has become an unlikely but dangerous focus of political debate – Islamophobic cartoons, homophobic pronouncements and sacrilegious depictions, glorification of terrorism and denial of the Holocaust. It seems like everyone is feeling pretty offended these days.

Academics, of course, think that if it causes offence it must be worth saying. Knowledge pushes boundaries, shakes things up and offends the complacency of received wisdom. No one has a right to be protected from offence, because all this challenging is good for us and good for society. As a result, things can be pretty lonely as we knock about being offensive in our ivory towers and/or crumbling lecture rooms, but we don't care because knowledge is more important than making friends.

As an example, the fairly unpopular campaign against the proposed terror bill has made much of the importance of academic freedom. We all know this drill – there can be no limit on free thought, even when that thought may cause offence, because once we authorise this censorship all learning is under threat. I really believe this. However much I may dislike some of what passes for academic work, I don't feel that it is safe to grant any external body power over what is and is not researched. There is always a danger that institutions of power will not approve of the business of learning – a business that may well call into question the basis and workings of power. Better by far to protect academic freedom and put up with the kinds of work that I don't much like.

What, then, of David Irving? Or Frank Ellis, the Leeds lecturer who happily tells the student paper that he believes that black people are inferior to whites and that he

agrees with repatriation? What about their academic freedom? And if I think that they are abusing the concept of free speech, why am I so uncomfortable about criminalising the glorification of terrorism?

Speech crimes protect the already powerful, because they are the people who can implement the law successfully

---

The jailing of David Irving is a difficult test for those of us who want to champion academic freedom. Holocaust denial is a particular and pernicious form of racism – one that rounds on the victims of extreme violence and genocide and implies that all that suffering, the pictures, the diaries, the bodies – all of it is a fabrication. See, the deniers say, this is how low these people will sink; they are so deceitful they even pretend to be dead. It is part of the literate racism that uses the veneer of respectable debate and, occasionally, scholarship, to argue that some people are lesser – less trustworthy, less intelligent, less human. If bad things happen to these creatures, it is no one's fault but their own.

I agree with David Cesarani when he says that Holocaust denial is not about asserting free speech – the point is to incite hatred and blur historical understanding so that doctrines of hatred can appear more respectable.

But I don't know how I can endorse the imprisonment of Irving for expressing hatred under the pretence of scholarship and still defend my own right to academic freedom. All kinds of things that I

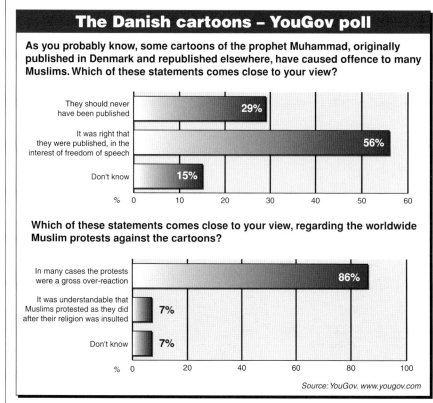

The Danish cartoons – YouGov poll

As you probably know, some cartoons of the prophet Muhammad, originally published in Denmark and republished elsewhere, have caused offence to many Muslims. Which of these statements comes close to your view?

- They should never have been published: 29%
- It was right that they were published, in the interest of freedom of speech: 56%
- Don't know: 15%

Which of these statements comes close to your view, regarding the worldwide Muslim protests against the cartoons?

- In many cases the protests were a gross over-reaction: 86%
- It was understandable that Muslims protested as they did after their religion was insulted: 7%
- Don't know: 7%

Source: YouGov. www.yougov.com

teach and research – about racism, sexuality, the exercise and abuse of global power – offend some and may be thought dangerous by others.

For those who believe that the West is under attack from the evil forces of terrorism, my attempts to contextualise attacks on so-called Western values as responses to longer histories of expropriation and exploitation may appear to be the equivalent of shouting 'fire' in a crowded theatre – too much freedom of speech, too little attention to dangerous consequences. I am not trying to offend, but where do we draw the line?

It isn't much help banning offensive speech if that just allows everyone to ignore offensive actions

---

The incidents in Leeds are slightly different. The comments made appear to be personal opinion and are not, to my knowledge, related to Ellis's area of academic expertise. Academic freedom cannot mean that academics have a right to espouse all kinds of inflammatory nonsense due to their status as academics. Equally, holding unpopular views should not, in itself, debar individuals from earning a living.

I want to believe that people can think what they like, as long as they keep fulfilling the demands of their job. I don't want to work alongside virulent racists, or have them teach my loved-ones and friends, or appraise my colleagues, or join my union – but I also don't want to persecute people for expressing unpopular or offensive views. I hope there is a proper investigation into how Ellis behaves in the workplace, but I also hope that the outcome is based on what he does, not what he says.

In the end, I think that speech crimes protect the already powerful, because they are the people who can implement the law successfully. The weak and vulnerable remain weak and vulnerable in relation to the law, and tend to be the ones who are hauled up on such charges as incitement.

Look at the discussion around the glorification of terrorism which has pointed again and again to the placards that appeared in early protests against the Danish cartoons of the prophet Muhammad. The outcry over these placards – which received considerable media coverage – has been used to argue that the offence of 'glorifying terrorism' is necessary and urgently so. As a result, in a climate of escalating racism against Muslims of all kinds, including those making endless efforts to show how moderate they are, public debate is focused on how very offensive and dangerous young Muslim men can be, rather than the dangerous racism of these cartoons and the climate in which they arise.

The slogans on placards may be stupid and insensitive – but are they really dangerous? Does anyone believe that it is these kinds of slogans that cause terrorism? Isn't there a world of difference between saying stupid things about violent acts and actually committing violence?

It is a hard one. Some things which offend me are just plain wrong. I don't think that those who deny the Holocaust or promote religiously inspired homophobia or celebrate white supremacy should be criminalised, but I also don't think that they should be allowed to use the education system to propagate their misguided views. Apart from anything else, it makes for rubbish education.

Academic freedom demands that a proper argument be put, not that any old nonsense be given airtime. At the same time, students and staff in universities need fair treatment and respect – if your colleague or lecturer makes it clear that they believe that you belong to a lesser species it is hard to see how they can maintain their professional responsibilities. However, that must be the test – how are you performing your professional responsibilities?

Much of the difficulty with dealing with the more mundane day-to-day racial discrimination in universities stems from this confusion between who you are and how you act. There is a general understanding that it is a bad thing to be called a racist, but little attention towards challenging and changing racially discriminatory actions.

Instead, whenever black and minority ethnic students and staff try to raise concerns about their treatment, this unleashes a torrent of defensive counterclaims because how dare anyone suggest that we are those despicable beings: 'racists'.

If we want to get rid of racism, we need to understand that it is a set of actions, not a state of being. It isn't much help banning offensive speech if that just allows everyone to ignore offensive actions.

I might not like what some people say, but I care far more about what they and their associates do.
15 March 2006

The Danish cartoon controversy

It is over four months since the Danish daily, Jyllands-Posten, printed twelve cartoons featuring the Muslim prophet Muhammad. The daily published the series of cartoons after Danish author Kåre Bluitgen complained that nobody dared illustrate his book about Muhammad, for fear of death threats similar to that endured by Salman Rushdie.

Islamic tradition bars pictorial depictions of the Prophet, although this oft-repeated injunction has on several occasions been breached before without causing controversy. Images circulating on the Internet now show bombs exploding over pictures of the newspaper, and blood flowing over the national flag and map of Denmark. What started out as a Danish journalistic project has now expanded into a global controversy.

The paper's Editor-in-Chief, Carsten Juste, said, 'We live in a democracy. That's why we can use all the journalistic methods we want to. Satire is accepted in this country, and you can make caricatures. Religion shouldn't set any barriers on that sort of expression. This doesn't mean that we wish to insult any Muslims.' He also said, 'We must quietly point out here that the drawings illustrated an article on the self-censorship which rules large parts of the Western world. Our right to say, write, photograph and draw what we want to within the framework of the law exists and must endure – unconditionally!'

He has now made a qualified apology: 'In our opinion, the 12 drawings were sober. They were not intended to be offensive, nor were they at variance with Danish law, but they have indisputably offended many Muslims for which we apologise.'

European newspapers, governments, the European Union, United Nations and Muslim organisations are now engulfed in the controversy, and the owner of *France Soir* has sacked the editor for publishing the cartoons.

The case has also been seized on by far-right groups to fuel race hatred, and, whilst certainly some of the papers which published the cartoons are politically conservative, this should not deter freedom of expression groups from stating their own positions clearly.

Freedom of opinion and expression is applicable not only to 'information' or 'ideas' that are favourably received, but also to those that offend, shock or disturb

---

There are important principles which need to be defended. One of these is that the right to freedom of opinion and expression is a fundamental right that safeguards the exercise of all other rights. It is a critical underpinning of democracy and applicable not only to 'information' or 'ideas' that are favourably received, but also to those that offend, shock or disturb.

Some of the cartoons published in the Danish paper may well be offensive to many Muslims (and may well be offensive to others, including cartoonists – some of the published cartoons are of poor quality), but charges of offence and blasphemy should not be deployed to curtail freedom of expression. The Campaign for Press and Broadcasting Freedom's position is that restrictions on freedom of expression which privilege certain ideas or beliefs cannot be justified.

European newspapers are also being put under unacceptable pressures, which can compromise the freedom of the press. Aidan White, General Secretary of the International Federation of Journalists, said that the dismissal of the editor of *France Soir*, Jacques Lefranc, 'sends a dangerous signal about unacceptable pressure on independent journalism'. The IFJ points out, 'Arab-world governments calling for political action against media are guilty of undue interference in the work of journalists.'

Clearly the row over the cartoons has dramatically revealed how fragile some of these important principles are. We need to avoid generating evermore anger and confrontation in this case, but at the same time restate firmly that freedom of expression and freedom of the press are important foundations of European democratic society and need to be strongly defended.
3 February 2006

■ The above information is reprinted with kind permission from the Campaign for Press and Broadcasting Freedom. Visit www.cpbf.org.uk for more information.
© CPBF

When speech offends

Questions and answers on the Danish cartoons and freedom of expression

On September 30, 2005, the Danish newspaper *Jyllands-Posten* published twelve cartoon depictions of the Prophet Muhammad that its editors said they solicited as part of an experiment to overcome what they perceived as self-censorship reflected in the reluctance of illustrators to depict the Prophet. The cartoons were highly offensive to Muslims because Islam is understood to prohibit graphic depictions of the Prophet and because most of the depictions were extremely derogatory, for example, by associating him, and by implication all Muslims, with terrorism.

At first protests against the cartoons extended little farther than Denmark's Muslim community, but by February 2006 an extraordinary outcry had spread to the Muslim world at large. Much of the outrage was directed against the government of Denmark, which, invoking its laws on freedom of expression, refused to suppress the cartoons or take action against their publishers. The Organization of the Islamic Conference, representing 57 countries, criticised Denmark for failing to apologize and take action against *Jyllands-Posten*, and is seeking a U.N. General Assembly resolution to ban attacks on religious beliefs. Mass protests have taken place in many countries, in some cases leading to violence, loss of life, and destruction of diplomatic and other property.

Jyllands-Posten, while apologising four months after publication for offending Muslims and denying any intent to incite a 'campaign' against them, defended its right to publish the cartoons. It reportedly received bomb threats that caused it to evacuate two offices in late January. Many other newspapers, in Europe and around the world, have reprinted the cartoons, sometimes as part of their reporting on the controversy and sometimes to reaffirm the right to publish material even if it offends religious views.

The cartoon controversy should be understood against a backdrop of rising Western prejudice and suspicion directed against Muslims, and an associated sense of persecution among Muslims in many parts of the world. In Europe, rapidly growing Muslim communities have become the continent's largest religious minority but also among its most economically disadvantaged communities and the target of discriminatory and anti-immigration measures. Acts of violence carried out in the name of radical Islamist groups coupled with parallel efforts to suppress that violence have aggravated tensions. So have disputes over the wars in Iraq and Afghanistan and continuing tensions in the Mideast over the Israeli-Palestinian conflict. In addition, several authoritarian governments in Muslim countries have seized on the cartoon controversy to deflect pressure from their own citizens for increased official accountability and respect for basic rights.

Much of the outrage against the cartoons has been framed not in terms of tangible acts of discrimination, violence or harassment against Muslims, but in terms of disrespect for Islam itself and those who adhere to it and animosity toward the Muslim world. Some have questioned why many nations in Europe, which continue to have blasphemy laws protecting the Christian religion, do not similarly protect Islam, or why anti-Semitic speech has been suppressed as 'hate speech' but not these cartoons. Western governments, in turn, have asked why governments of predominantly Muslim nations are so outraged over the cartoons' disparagement of Islam when they permit similarly disrespectful commentary about members of other religions or religious sects in their official press.

Western governments have resisted suppressing or punishing publication of the cartoons, but governments in predominantly Muslim countries, including Jordan and Yemen, have arrested and brought criminal charges against editors whose papers reprinted the cartoons. Malaysia on February 9 declared it an offence for anyone to publish, produce, import, circulate or possess the caricatures.

As detailed below, Human Rights Watch rejects the disrespectful and prejudiced attitudes reflected in the cartoons, but affirms that, under the right of freedom of expression, governments are not entitled to suppress speech simply because it is offensive or disrespectful of religion. Still, we recognise that for many the cartoon controversy raises difficult questions. We post below our effort to answer those questions.

What does international human rights law tell us about the dispute over the cartoons?

International human rights law cannot answer all questions raised about the cartoons. Human rights law obliges governments to protect religious freedom and religious minorities, but, as explained below, the cartoon controversy mostly concerns the limits imposed by human rights law, particularly the right to freedom of expression, on governments' ability to suppress speech. In prohibiting governmental censorship of certain kinds of speech, human rights law does not suggest endorsement of that speech. Similarly, while the right to freedom of expression requires governments to allow speech that they and many others might find offensive, misguided, or even immoral, human rights law cannot answer the question of whether it was wise or proper for *Jyllands-Posten* and others to publish the cartoons. Nor can human rights law dictate the posture that governments should take toward the cartoons in their public comments – whether, for example, they should clarify that the content does not reflect official views or express their belief that it was unwise to have used the freedom of expression in this way. Rather, human rights law, in relevant part, speaks only to whether governments must permit such speech, regardless of whether they endorse the views expressed.

The cartoons caused extreme offence to many Muslims – why should the right to freedom of expression protect such cartoons?
The right to freedom of expression is a fundamental one, necessary to protect the exercise of all other human rights in democratic societies because it is essential for holding governments accountable to the public. Freedom of expression is particularly necessary with respect to provocative or offensive speech, because once governmental censorship is permitted in such cases, the temptation is enormous for government officials to find speech that is critical of them to be unduly provocative or offensive as well. The freedom to express even controversial points of view is also important for societies to address key political, social, and cultural issues, since taboos often mask matters of considerable public concern that

are best addressed through honest and unfettered debate among those holding diverse points of view. Although international human rights law does impose certain limits on the right to freedom of expression (discussed below), the important functions served by that right require interpreting those limitations narrowly.

Advocacy of religious hatred can be suppressed only when it constitutes imminent incitement to unlawful acts of discrimination, hostility or violence

---

Aren't pictures as hateful as these properly considered 'hate speech'?
Not all speech that is hateful constitutes 'hate speech' that must be prohibited under international human rights law. Advocacy of religious hatred can be suppressed only when it constitutes imminent incitement to unlawful acts of discrimination, hostility or violence. In addition, to constitute such incitement, the discrimination, hostility or violence must be urged or promoted by the speech in question. It is not incitement when opponents of speech or those who find the speech offensive use violence, since that would give censorship over any speech to those who are willing to employ violence to attack it. In this case, the main complaint against the cartoons is that they offend Islam, not that they have inspired acts of violence, criminal harassment or tangible discrimination against Danish or other Muslims. Speech that targets a religion for disrespect, as opposed to speech that targets believers for unlawful acts, is protected, however offensive it may be.

Why not ban the cartoons as blasphemy?
Many European nations still have blasphemy laws, although they are seldom enforced. Some of these laws

prohibit blasphemy against only certain religions, such as Christianity. Such laws are clearly discriminatory and may reflect broader societal discrimination. Moreover, many of these laws should not be on the books at all. Although the European Court of Human Rights has upheld some of these laws, it is far from clear why certain religious beliefs should be protected from critical discussion or even ridicule when other political beliefs, aesthetic views, or cultural opinions are not. Freedom of expression is valuable for allowing broad public debate of any topic. It is wrong to exclude from that debate certain religious beliefs, because speech on these topics is about ideas, not incitement or even advocacy of violence.

Isn't it inconsistent for European governments to criminalise private speech that is anti-Semitic, including speech that denies the Holocaust, but refuse to criminalise the private publication of the cartoons, on free speech grounds?
Human Rights Watch recognises that the tragedy of the Holocaust is the historical context in which laws banning Holocaust denial were adopted in several European countries, as well as in Israel. We also acknowledge that, by more rigorously enforcing these laws, some governments have sought to underscore the seriousness with which they view the danger posed by right-wing extremists and others who deny such events. Such laws were also motivated by a desire not to exacerbate the suffering of Holocaust

survivors living in these countries. As noted above, however, prohibiting speech, such as Holocaust denial, that is offensive or distressing to some religions or minorities, while tolerating speech that is offensive or distressing to others, is a clearly discriminatory practice and raises legitimate questions about double standards.

As Human Rights Watch stated in 1995, we believe that all such laws, regardless of the religions or minorities they seek to protect, disproportionately restrict the protected right to freedom of expression. We are mindful that there are different perspectives on what is permissible and prohibited speech, but we base our position on a strong commitment to freedom of expression as a core principle of human rights and our conviction that objectionable speech is best met with contrary speech, not censorship. We also believe that governments can best counter offensive speech by fulfilling their obligation to take positive measures to protect minorities and to make clear that they reject all forms of discrimination.

Prohibiting denial of the Holocaust may be popular politically, but Human Rights Watch is also concerned that over the long run, such measures are not effective to counter bigotry, and may even be counterproductive. Draconian bans may turn bigots into victims, driving them underground and creating a more attractive home for those who are drawn to such groups.

Why can't the cartoons be banned as potentially harmful to public safety or the rights of Muslims?
Freedom of expression may be limited to protect public safety and the rights of others, but such limitations must be strictly 'necessary' in a democratic society. Banning provocative speech rarely meets that test. In the case of the cartoons, any threat of violence by protesters should be contained through traditional law enforcement means. In some countries where protests have turned violent, however, officials seem to have tolerated the unlawful behavior – a disregard of their responsibilities that makes it

all the more inappropriate to blame the original cartoons for ensuing unrest. A society built on respect for freedom of expression and the value of robust debate should, wherever possible, meet offensive speech with more speech – denunciations, objections, explanations – rather than censorship in the name of public safety.

Editors should be held responsible for what they decide to publish – but by their readers, communities, or employers, not their governments

---

As for the rights of Muslims, the cartoons in no sense impede Muslims' right to freedom of religion. Religious freedom means that all people have the liberty to adopt the religious beliefs (or non-beliefs) of their choosing and to worship and, as much as possible in a democratic society, live their own lives in accordance with those beliefs. However, freedom of religion does not give anyone the right to impose his or her religious beliefs on others. That Muslims find the depictions of the Prophet Muhammad objectionable does not give them the right under international human rights law to insist that others abide by their views. Muslims, like all others, are free to state their religious objections and to

press for more respectful treatment, but they are not entitled to censor the expression of others in the name of their own religious freedom.

Why shouldn't the government hold editors responsible for publishing such offensive material?
Editors should be held responsible for what they decide to publish – but by their readers, communities, or employers, not their governments. Under the right of freedom of expression, a government cannot impose its views of what is fit to publish except in very limited cases as described above.

Don't Muslims and everyone offended by the cartoons have the right to protest them?
Human rights law protects the right to peacefully protest offensive speech, just as it protects the right to utter provocative or offensive speech. Governments have a duty to make peaceful protest possible, by respecting the right of individuals to assemble, express outrage, organise boycotts, and engage in other peaceful acts. Governments also have a duty to protect the public from protests that turn violent, to take appropriate action against specific threats against the life and property of others, and to reaffirm their own duty to avoid discriminatory speech and actions.
15 February 2006

■ The above information is reprinted with kind permission from Human Rights Watch. Visit www.hrw.org for more information.
© Human Rights Watch

Your right to protest

Learn about your right to protest, and non-violent direct action. By Martin Burrows

The history of protesting

Civil protesting has been around in one form or another for many hundreds of years. The Tolpuddle Martyrs were carted off to Australia in 1830 for protesting about rich landowners, while Wat Tyler, in 1381, led the original poll tax protestors pre-empting the 1990 protestors by over 500 years. Tyler's band were captured and put to death, their objectives unrealised while the 1990ers had an afternoon of rioting and the bill was abolished. Mind you they did have Julian Cope on their side, dressed as an eight-foot space alien.

While protests like the May Day riots in London and the protests against the WTO (World Trade Organisation) in the United States and Geneva tend to grab the headlines for all the wrong reasons there has been an emphasis towards peaceful protesting or non-violent direct action (NVDA) as it is also called.

What is peaceful protesting or NVDA?

It means that you can take part in public protest but that it does not involve violence against property or persons, whether they are rival protestors, objects of your protest or the police. The point of peaceful protesting is to get your point across whether that is to like-minded others or what is deemed as the opposition. It can be extremely effective as it gets excellent media coverage, increases awareness of your campaign and encourages others to join your campaign.

What you can do as part of NVDA

■ You can take part in or organise a rally, march or assembly. But as an organiser you must seek permission from the police first stating how many people you expect to turn up, time and place and the route of a march;

TheSite.org

■ A sit-in;
■ A blockade;
■ You can run a stall, but you must seek permission from your local council first before doing so.

Can I still be arrested?

Yes, even on a peaceful protest. A sit-down protest or a blockade even with absence of violence can be construed as obstruction as can blocking the streets, pavements or buildings. Chanting racist remarks or remarks likely to incite violence will also lead to arrest.

Jason Green has been involved in both peaceful and violent confront-ational protests. He has protested on behalf of Reclaim the Streets, gone on anti-capitalism marches, and has been a hunt saboteur.

'While there is something to be said for confrontational or violent protesting, I think that it is very short-termist, it attracts a bad element and it gets such bad publicity. I think that the May Day riots while showing that so many people are angry also overshadowed the people who were peacefully protesting. Given the choice I would now rather use NVDA methods.'

Pressure groups like the League against Cruel Sports, CND, and Drop the Debt have long been advocates of peaceful protests. Drop the Debt have been so successful that governments have now dropped many of the crippling debts owed by the poorer countries of the world.

'Drop the Debt condemns any form of violence. Supporters come for a peaceful and positive march to send a clear message to the G8 to cancel more debt. The debt burden in the poorest countries has been a central issue at the G8 annual summits since 70,000 peaceful campaigners filled the streets of Birmingham in May 1998. Amidst the security concerns and speculation, the G8 must take on the criticisms of peaceful campaigners.'

■ The above information is re-printed with kind permission from TheSite.org. Please visit www. thesite.org for more information.

© *TheSite.org*

Double standards in freedom of expression

Information from the *Muslim News*

By Sadiq Khan

It is an interesting time for debates on the freedom of expression. Last month, key clauses of the Government's Racial and Religious Hatred Bill were defeated in the Commons. The Bill brings in a new offence of incitement to religious hatred, but the version that passed was considerably weaker than originally intended, and it is now doubtful whether it will be strong enough to curb the activities of the far right stirring up hatred against Muslims. At the same time, existing race hate legislation was put to test in the trial of the Leader of the BNP, who was found not guilty, despite video evidence of him describing Islam as a 'wicked, vicious faith.' In the following week, Abu Hamza Al Masri was found guilty of inciting racial hatred against Jews (as well as even more serious offences). Although both of these men are despicable and unsavoury to the vast majority of the community they claim to represent, they do illustrate why there is a feeling of injustice and double standards with regards to freedom of expression. Our laws are being tested, as well as our tolerance over the limits of acceptable speech and behaviour.

At the same time, the controversy over the publication of cartoons depicting Prophet Muhammad (peace be upon him) rages on around the world, and shows little sign of abating. At the time of writing, over a dozen protestors against the cartoons have died in Afghanistan, which is surely an indication that the situation has lost all sense of proportion, and that those pitched on either side of the debate are incapable of listening to calls for calm or indeed, to each other.

There is no doubt in my mind that the publication of the cartoons in the Danish newspaper, *Jyllands*

Posten, back in September, and their subsequent reproduction in newspapers across Europe, showed an extraordinary lack of judgement and understanding. They were gratuitously offensive, tasteless and provocative – and extremely Islamophobic and racist. Attempts have been made to defend the publication of the cartoons, pointing to the lack of comprehension from non-Muslims about the offence caused in depicting the Prophet. Ignorance is no defence in this case, and the fact that the Danish paper actively invited people to contribute cartoons as a dare suggests that the editors were well aware of what they were doing. Islamic tradition explicitly prohibits any depiction of Allah (God) and the Prophet.

There is a feeling of injustice and double standards with regards to freedom of expression

It is also the case that any discussion of the cartoons cannot be taken in a vacuum, or isolated from the wider context of how minority religions live in Western societies, whilst keeping their faith.

There is first the context of Denmark to consider. This is a country where an extreme right-wing party (The Danish People's Party) is the third largest, and advocates an anti-immigration stance. Many of the country's 170,000 Muslims feel a strong sense of marginalisation and under-representation. Although it took nearly four months for the controversy to spread to other

European countries, and further afield, it is easy to pick out a common theme – a growing feeling of impotence, discrimination and lack of power amongst Muslims. In a situation where many feel they have no control or say in domestic or international events, cartoons that dehumanise (in the same way that cartoons in the 1930s were used by the Nazis to stereotype, and justify discrimination, and ultimately genocide against Jews), insult and gratuitously offend a prophet inexorably connected to the religion of Islam and revered and loved by all Muslims, touch a raw nerve. Protest is a way of expressing anger at the Islamophobia that is so acutely felt and experienced on a daily basis.

However, nothing can justify Danish embassies being burnt, placards being held in a demonstration celebrating the July bombers and demanding beheadings, or people dying over this issue. It is also depressing to hear that Iranian newspapers are publishing cartoons of the Holocaust, in a counter-productive 'tit for tat' move.

In the UK, the placards were held by a small fringe element within the Muslim community, and in comparison to other demonstrations that have been held on the streets of London in living memory, was relatively muted. The wider perception is that the controversy of the cartoons has been hijacked for a larger purpose – to highlight a 'clash of civilisations' between the Muslim world and the West. So it rests on more responsible members of our faith to explain why the cartoons were offensive, and talk about the underlying issues behind the reaction from Muslims in a calm and measured way.

The publication of these caricatures of Prophet Muhammad (p)

add insult to injury to the millions of Muslims in all four corners of the world who experience huge injustices. Notwithstanding this, it is worth reminding ourselves of the example of Prophet Muhammad (p) and his reaction to things that faced him – when faced with verbal abuse, personal attacks and threats to his life – he did not behave in the way that a small fringe element have.

In Europe, we have a separation between government and the press and this means that whilst on one hand, the press plays a vital role in holding government to account, the flipside is that the government does not and cannot censor what is published in newspapers. It is worth bearing in mind the advantage of this. Would we really want a government being able to stop a newspaper publishing a damaging story about, for example, government corruption? Or to stop cartoons satirising a politician's behaviour? However, the cartoon caricatures of Prophet Muhammed (p) are a million miles from this. Whilst not suggesting the criminal prosecution of the publishers, surely there is a responsibility to act maturely and show self-restraint? What public interest did publication serve? What news story did it help illustrate?

This issue has highlighted the need for responsibility and caution in exercising so-called 'freedom of expression'. In a context where the press can publish whatever it likes, there must be a presumption that a sense of reason and tolerance will prevail, being aware of good taste and what will be taken as provocative and unacceptable. We can endlessly debate where the limits of self-censorship are, and probably never reach a consensus. Thankfully, in the UK so far our press has been mature and understanding on this issue, in marked contrast to some papers and magazines elsewhere in Europe who have used dubious justifications to reproduce the cartoons.

There is, of course, an irony. Some of the countries where the press have chosen to make a stand for free speech, and print the cartoons, have laws, which (rightly) provide that denying the Holocaust is a criminal offence. Many Muslims are asking the question is this irony or overt double standards.

Mainstream Muslim organisations should be praised for the speed with which they unequivocally condemned the placard-holding protestors and the man who thought it was clever to imitate a suicide bomber in London. But we now have a much larger task ahead to continue to promote a more positive public image of Muslims in the UK and the West following the controversy over these cartoons. Neither Muslims nor the West should demonise each other. Both need to curb extremism and promote moderation. Our responsibility is not to allow issues that are dear to us to be taken to extremes by fringe elements of the community. The silent majority can no longer be silent any more. Those who protest, and those who are in uproar about the right of freedom of expression also need to develop tolerance and understanding which acknowledges cultural differences. Given the intransigence that both sides have displayed, backtracking to a rational debate and discussion seems a daunting task, but is not one that we should shy away from under any circumstances.

Sadiq Khan is MP for Tooting
24 February 2006

■ Reprinted with permission from *Muslim News*. Visit www.muslimnews.co.uk for more.

© Muslim News

The blasphemy law

A briefing paper from the Campaign Against Censorship

1) Blasphemy is not a statutory offence. The Blasphemy Act was repealed in 1969.
2) Blasphemy remains a common law offence. It involves 'any contemptuous, reviling, scurrilous or ludicrous matter relating to God, Jesus Christ, the Bible or the formularies of the Church of England as by law established'.
3) This is clearly discriminatory in that it covers (i) no religion other than Christianity and (ii) no sect other than the Church of England.
4) Two possible remedies have been suggested: (i) extension of the law to cover other religions and other sects or (ii) total abolition.
5) The law cannot logically be extended to other religions. Muslims and Jews regard the basic claims of Christianity as blasphemous. Christians return the compliment. Buddhists do not worship a 'god' at all. The problem of definition is not solvable.
6) To extend the law to other sects would (i) provide opportunity and ammunition for sects to attack each other at the expense of the already overloaded legal system and (ii) offer the protection of the law to 'fringe' organisations whose methods and motives are highly suspect.
7) The law discriminates against people (atheists and agnostics) whose convictions are just as strongly held as those of religious believers but who refuse to subscribe to any religion. Any extension would make it worse.
8) The only fair, practical, and sensible course is to abolish the law of blasphemy altogether.
9) The CAC supports and will work for complete abolition of the law of blasphemy.
10) The CAC opposes and will resist future attempts to impose constraints on freedom of religion, including the freedom to have none.

■ The above information is reprinted with kind permission from the Campaign Against Censorship. Visit www.dlas.org.uk for more information.

© Campaign Against Censorship

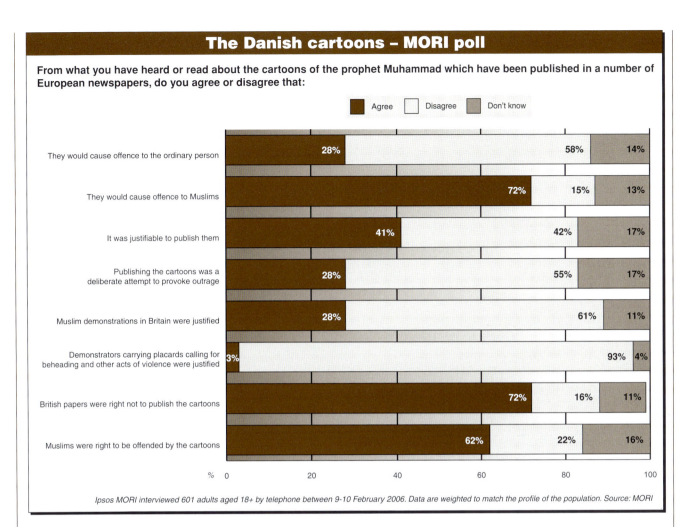

The Danish cartoons – MORI poll

From what you have heard or read about the cartoons of the prophet Muhammad which have been published in a number of European newspapers, do you agree or disagree that:

Legend: Agree · Disagree · Don't know

	Agree	Disagree	Don't know
They would cause offence to the ordinary person	28%	58%	14%
They would cause offence to Muslims	72%	15%	13%
It was justifiable to publish them	41%	42%	17%
Publishing the cartoons was a deliberate attempt to provoke outrage	28%	55%	17%
Muslim demonstrations in Britain were justified	28%	61%	11%
Demonstrators carrying placards calling for beheading and other acts of violence were justified	3%	93%	4%
British papers were right not to publish the cartoons	72%	16%	11%
Muslims were right to be offended by the cartoons	62%	22%	16%

Ipsos MORI interviewed 601 adults aged 18+ by telephone between 9-10 February 2006. Data are weighted to match the profile of the population. Source: MORI

The government and the media

Who rules?

The media are powerful tools. If you know how to use them well you can make situations work to your advantage. The government knows just how influential the media can be, so constantly it has to think about how to use the media carefully.

Political parties and the government have special media and publicity departments that deal with their public image and decide what news should be released and when. They even decide how politicians should look and dress, what they should say and when and how they should say it – even what expressions they should pull. It's all about getting the right message across to potential voters.

Spinning the news

Imagine the government has decided it needs to increase tax. The public isn't going to be happy, but it needs to be informed. Once the media get hold of this news it's likely to be splashed over the front pages.

The government will probably look really bad, especially if it promised not to increase tax, so a spin doctor looks at the situation and decides the government should wait for a bigger news story to come along. So it waits... and the country wins an important football match. Perfect time to release the story.

The papers are full of football, nobody thinks much about other news and anyway, who cares? The government's news is buried away where nobody notices. It's all very clever. Has the prime minister done something not entirely truthful? It will help if on the day the story appears that the prime minister is seen to be visiting sick children. This will divert attention away from bad news.

Key points

- The government needs the media to get its message across.
- Political parties have special departments that deal with their public image.
- Spin doctors are special advisers to politicians and governments. They help position the news so that the government appears in the best light.

Reality bytes: a spin too far?

After the events of 11 September in the US, the news covered little else. There was huge demand for stories about what had happened, why it had happened and what might happen in the future. A special adviser thought this was the perfect opportunity for the UK government to deliver any bad news, because it was unlikely to get noticed.

She suggested this in an email to her colleagues. The email was discovered and caused outrage. The adviser had to make a public apology and in the end had to resign. However, this incident exposed to the public a practice that has been happening for some time.

Interesting facts

- Parliament was first televised in 1985. The first broadcasts were of the House of Lords. Televising the House of Commons followed in 1989.

- The government is considering restricting adverts for junk food to after 9pm in order to encourage healthy eating.

Big question

- Should the media be banned from expressing political opinions?

- Information from Channel 4. Visit www.channel4.com for more information.

© Channel 4

The Internet

Is freedom of speech a right, or sometimes a wrong?

The Internet means that all of our voices can be heard across the world. But should some voices be heard whilst others should be censored? And if they should be censored, where should the line be drawn?

A right

The argument for freedom of speech is simple: it's a basic right of everyone on this planet.

We should never forget people such as Nelson Mandela, Malcolm X and Martin Luther King who fought to give a voice to people who couldn't shout loud enough themselves – and changed humanity in the process.

The development of news broadcasting over the years has helped bring the plight of suffering nations into the public domain but it has always been limited. News is nearly always controlled by businessmen or governments and therefore affected by political whim and economic agendas.

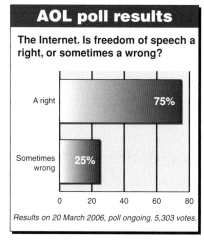

AOL poll results

The Internet. Is freedom of speech a right, or sometimes a wrong?

A right — 75%
Sometimes wrong — 25%

0 20 40 60 80

Results on 20 March 2006, poll ongoing. 5,303 votes.

But the Internet is free from these constraints and acts as a genuine loudspeaker for people's opinions, whoever and wherever they are. And because the Internet is accessible in every corner of the globe – and growing fast – it reaches more people than any other medium. Add to this that it is mostly uncensored – leaving people free to voice their opinions without fear – and it's clear the Internet is the most perfect example of true democratic communication.

From politics to arts, music to public affairs – the Internet creates true freedom of speech around the globe.

Sometimes wrong

We take it for granted that freedom of speech is a good thing. But is it?

The world has changed and the birth of the Internet means we need to rethink what freedom of speech actually means. Do we really want racist propaganda and religious hatred in our homes? Not to mention pornographic material – some of which, tragically, includes children.

It's not an issue that can be ignored – this affects our daily lives. The Internet was recently used by religious fundamentalists to incite hatred prior to the 7/7 bombings in London. And although there's no definite link between the Internet and terrorism, it's a fact that any web user is just a few clicks away from instructions on how to make a bomb.

The world has changed and the birth of the Internet means we need to rethink what freedom of speech actually means. Do we really want racist propaganda and religious hatred in our homes?

And it doesn't stop there. The Internet's been used to promote every kind of evil from online suicide pacts to eating disorders. There are even sites that promote self-harm which is fast becoming a worrying new trend among western teenagers.

It's true that the Internet's here to stay but why let it endanger our lives – and threaten our children's safety? Isn't it time our governments did something to stop this happening? Censorship is the only answer.

- The above information is reprinted with kind permission from AOL. Visit www.aol.co.uk/discuss for more information.

© AOL

Internet companies 'must respect free speech'

Reporters without Borders has called on companies such as Microsoft and Yahoo to respect human rights, even if the countries they are operating in don't. By Andrew Donoghue

IT companies operating in countries with repressive regimes should face tighter regulation when it comes to supporting freedom of speech, according to a leading anti-censorship organisation.

Press freedom group Reporters without Borders issued a report late last week calling on the US government and US regulators to help develop a voluntary code of conduct for IT companies operating in countries such as China, Tunisia and Burma.

Yahoo signed an agreement with the Chinese government back in 2002, agreeing to censor the results of the Chinese version of its search engine

One recommendation made by the group is that US companies should be prevented from hosting email servers in countries with repressive regimes. This would ensure that any requests for information from the authorities of a repressive regime would have to pass through the US judicial system, the group claims.

'We believe these practices violate the rights to freedom of expression as defined in article 19 of the Universal Declaration of Human Rights. Such ethical failings on the part of American companies damage the image of the United States abroad,' said the Reporters without Borders statement.

www.zdnet.co.uk

The group claimed that a law regulating the activities of Internet companies should be a last resort but would become necessary if a code of conduct cannot be agreed by a specific deadline.

The publication of the Reporters without Borders document follows recent condemnation of Microsoft and Yahoo's activities in China.

Earlier this month it emerged that Microsoft had agreed to remove the blog of a Chinese journalist from its MSN Spaces site. The software maker claimed that the site was blocked to help ensure the service complied with local laws in China.

'Microsoft is a multi-national business and as such needs to manage the reality of operating in countries around the world,' a Microsoft spokesperson said at the time.

Yahoo signed an agreement with the Chinese government back in 2002, agreeing to censor the results of the Chinese version of its search engine. More recently, according to Reporters without Borders, Yahoo had cooperated with Chinese authorities to identify and convict a pro-human rights journalist in China.

In 2004, Reporters without Borders criticised both Yahoo and Google for complicity with the Chinese authorities for blocking 'subversive' content, and called for the US government to protect the rights of Chinese web users.
10 January 2006

■ The above information is reprinted with kind permission from ZDNet. Visit www.zdnet.co.uk for more information.

Backlash as Google shores up great firewall of China

By Jonathan Watts in Jinan

- *US search engine agrees to government restrictions*
- *Firm admits inconsistency with its corporate ethics*

The following correction was printed in the *Guardian's* Corrections and clarifications column, Saturday January 28 2006.

In the article below we described Falun Gong as a cult. In doing so, we should have made clear that we were giving the Chinese government's official view of the movement.

Google, the world's biggest search engine, will team up with the world's biggest censor, China, today with a service that it hopes will make it more attractive to the country's 110 million online users.

After holding out longer than any other major Internet company, Google will effectively become another brick in the great firewall of China when it starts filtering out information that it believes the government will not approve of.

Despite a year of soul-searching, the American company will join Microsoft and Yahoo! in helping the communist government block access to websites containing politically sensitive content, such as references to the Tiananmen Square massacre and criticism of the politburo.

Executives have grudgingly accepted that this is the ethical price they have to pay to base servers in mainland China, which will improve the speed – and attractiveness – of their service in a country where they face strong competition from the leading mandarin search engine, Baidu.

But Google faces a backlash from free speech advocates, Internet activists and politicians, some of whom are already asking how the company's policy in China accords with its mission statement: to make all possible information available to everyone who has a computer or mobile phone.

The new interface – google.cn – started at midnight last night and will be slowly phased in over the coming months. Although users will have the option of continuing to search via the original US-based google.com website, it is expected that the vast majority of Chinese search enquiries will go through mainland-based servers.

> *Google, the world's biggest search engine, will team up with the world's biggest censor, China, with a service that it hopes will make it more attractive to the country's 110 million online users*

This will require the company to abide by the rules of the world's most restricted Internet environment. China is thought to have 30,000 online police monitoring blogs, chatrooms and news portals. The propaganda department is thought to employ even more people, a small but increasing number of whom are paid to anonymously post pro-government comments online. Sophisticated filters have been developed to block or limit access to 'unhealthy information', which includes human rights websites, such as Amnesty, foreign news outlets, such as the BBC, as well as pornography. Of the 64 Internet dissidents in prison worldwide, 54 are from China.

Google has remained outside this system until now. But its search results are still filtered and delayed by the giant banks of government servers, known as the great firewall of China. Type 'Falun Gong' in the search engine from a Beijing computer and the only results that can be accessed are official condemnations.

Now, however, Google will actively assist the government to limit content. There are technical

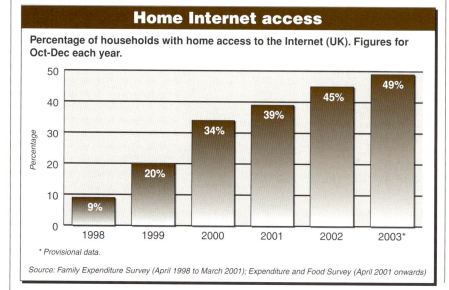

Home Internet access

Percentage of households with home access to the Internet (UK). Figures for Oct-Dec each year.

- 1998: 9%
- 1999: 20%
- 2000: 34%
- 2001: 39%
- 2002: 45%
- 2003*: 49%

* Provisional data.

Source: Family Expenditure Survey (April 1998 to March 2001); Expenditure and Food Survey (April 2001 onwards)

precedents. In Germany, Google follows government orders by restricting references to sites that deny the Holocaust. In France, it obeys local rules prohibiting sites that stir up racial hatred. And in the US, it assists the authorities' crackdown on copyright infringements.

Google will effectively become another brick in the great firewall of China when it starts filtering out information that it believes the government will not approve of

---

The scale of censorship in China is likely to dwarf anything the company has done before. According to one Internet media insider, the main taboos are the three Ts: Tibet, Taiwan and the Tiananmen massacre, and the two Cs: cults such as Falun Gong and criticism of the Communist party. But this list is frequently updated.

In a statement, Google said it had little choice: 'To date, our search service has been offered exclusively from outside China, resulting in latency and access issues that have been unsatisfying to our Chinese users and, therefore, unacceptable to Google. With google.cn, Chinese users will ultimately receive a search service that is fast, always accessible, and helps them find information both in China and from around the world.'

It acknowledged that this is contrary to its corporate ethics, but said a greater good was served by providing information in China. 'In order to operate from China, we have removed some content from the search results available on google.cn, in response to local law, regulation or policy. While removing search results is inconsistent with Google's mission, providing no information (or a heavily degraded user experience that amounts to no information) is more inconsistent with our mission.'

Initially, Google will not use Chinese servers for two of its most popular services: Gmail and blogger. This is a reflection of the company's discomfort with the harsh media environment – and the subsequent risks to its corporate image.

In an attempt to be more transparent than its rivals, Google said it would inform users that certain web pages had been removed from the list of results on the orders of the government. But its motivation is economic: a chunk of the fast-growing Chinese search market, estimated to be worth $151m (£84m) in 2004. This is still small by US standards, but with the number of web users increasing at the rate of more than 20 million a year, the online population is on course to overtake the US within the next decade.

Julian Pain of Reporters Without Borders – a freedom of expression advocacy group that also has its website blocked in China – accused Google of hypocrisy. 'This is very bad news for the Internet in China. Google were the only ones who held out. So the Chinese government had

to block information themselves. But now Google will do it for them,' he said. 'They have two standards. One for the US, where they resist government demands for personal information, and one for China, where they are helping the authorities block thousands of websites.'

Local bloggers were already wearily resigned to the change. 'What Google are doing is targeting commercial interests and skirting political issues,' said one of the country's most prominent, who writes under the name Black Hearted Killer. 'That by itself is no cause for criticism, but there is no doubt they are cowards.'

Forbidden searches

Words or phrases that can trigger pages to be blocked or removed from search results:

Tiananmen Square massacre
The killing of hundreds, if not thousands, of civilians by the People's Liberation Army in 1989

Dalai Lama
The exiled spiritual leader of Tibet, who is denounced as a splittist by the government in Beijing

Taiwanese independence
The nightmare of the Communist party, which has vowed to use force to prevent a breakaway

Falun Gong
A banned spiritual movement, thousands of whose members have been imprisoned and in many cases tortured

Dongzhou
The village where paramilitary police shot and killed at least three protesters last month.
25 January 2005

Censorship and regulation

How the powers that be control film and TV content

It is perhaps a tribute (though a backhanded one) to the power of the moving image that it should be subject to far greater censorship than any other artistic medium. Current technology makes it effectively impossible to censor the written word, theatre censorship was abolished in 1968, and there has never been any systematic regulation of other art forms – anyone seeking to clamp down on such events must mount a private prosecution, a lengthy and expensive process.

Film and video releases in Britain are amongst the most tightly-regulated in the Western world

However, film and video releases in Britain are amongst the most tightly-regulated in the Western world. With only a few exceptions, every commercially-released film both in cinemas and on video will have been vetted by the British Board of Film Classification (originally founded in 1912 as the British Board of Film Censors), which applies age-restrictive classifications and, in some cases, recommends cutting or otherwise altering the film in order to conform to their guidelines.

These guidelines are based on two main factors: legal requirements (for instance, unsimulated animal cruelty, indecent images of children) and the BBFC's own policies. The latter have changed enormously over the last century, ranging from rigidly applied lists of forbidden topics to the current context-based system where artistic merit is a key factor in assessing individual films.

Though this approach has undoubtedly led to a number of important films being passed either uncut or with a milder age restriction than one would expect, it is also controversial, due to the inevitable inconsistency. Some films are treated much more leniently than others with very similar content, as a result of largely subjective judgements by a handful of people.

Contrary to popular belief, the BBFC is not a government organisation. In fact, central government has no direct involvement in film censorship beyond passing legislation affecting the BBFC's activities. Local authorities have considerably more power, including the final say in whether or not certain films can be shown, though in the vast majority of cases they are happy to accept the BBFC's verdict. Indeed, this is why the BBFC was created by the film industry in the first place.

The history of British film censorship is as much social as cultural: the reasons films were banned in the 1920s (revolutionary politics) and 1950s (nudity) say as much about the society of the time as anything in the films. It is also revealing that in an era of far greater equality the BBFC is noticeably tougher on sexual violence today than it was thirty years ago, though correspondingly much more relaxed about most other issues.

As technology develops, the BBFC's role may well become less and less significant. A side-effect of its stated commitment to greater openness is that it is now easy to find out if films have been cut in their British versions and current technology makes it equally simple to order uncut and unclassified videos and DVDs from elsewhere (such material cannot be legally sold within the UK, but there are no barriers to importation). If this practice becomes widespread enough to affect the British film industry economically, it is likely that pressure will be applied on the BBFC to reflect this.

■ The above information is reprinted with kind permission from screenonline. Visit www.screenonline.org.uk for more information.

© *The British Film Institute*

Classified material

**Film censorship: it's there for a reason. So what needs to be cut?
Joanna Scott delves into the ratings system of the BBFC**

Throughout cinematic history there have always been films that caused a storm. Some films – usually involving scenes of sex or violence – have provoked such a level of controversy that protesters have picketed cinemas and local authorities have been forced to ban the movies.

The ensuing ruckus in the media merely reminds us that we live in a society that is censored. In the seventies, films such as *Straw Dogs* and *A Clockwork Orange* raised controversy because they contained scenes that linked sex and violence.

It was not so long ago that Westminster Council banned David Cronenberg's *Crash* and Bournemouth Council did likewise with Catherine Breillat's *Romance* – because of the sexual content particular to both films.

Legal eagles

Occasionally the government has stepped in. After the tabloid press coined the term 'video nasty' and campaigned against unclassified video release in the early eighties (at the time around 60 titles had already been prosecuted under the Obscene Publications Act or were awaiting prosecution), new legislation was introduced to control home entertainment distribution.

As well as sex, violence and horror, religion too, can prove to be a taboo subject. Martin Scorsese's *The Last Temptation of Christ* as well as Monty Python's *The Life of Brian* caused a public outcry in Ireland; and Mel Gibson's *The Passion of the Christ* is the latest film to hit the headlines, with debate even reaching the inner sanctum of the Vatican.

There are also more subtle forms of censorship which most of us never hear about. For example, *Star Wars: Episode II – Attack of the Clones* received a one-second cut of a head-butt while the distributor of *Lara Croft: Tomb Raider* had to delete scenes involving throat chops.

Had young children watched these moves there was a concern they might attempt to imitate them.

Decision makers

So who is responsible for making these content decisions? In the early 1900s responsibility for film classification lay in the hands of local authorities but the film industry found this problematic because they would receive different ratings from the numerous local authorities.

So the British Board of Film Censors (BBFC), an independent non-profit-making body (funded by fees), was established by the film industry in 1912 to bring consistency to classification.

After the tabloid press campaigned against unclassified video release in the early eighties, new legislation was introduced to control home entertainment distribution

On the whole, local authorities accepted the decisions of the BBFC though they retained statutory powers giving them the right to overrule the Board's decisions at any time.

In 1984 the Video Recordings Act came into force and the BBFC was also designated the official body to classify all home videos (as well as DVDs now).

In addition, the BBFC's name was updated to the British Board of Film Classification to reflect the fact that classification plays a far larger part in the Board's work than censorship.

But do we still feel censorship is enforced upon us?

'People shouldn't feel that they're having their viewing censored, 'says BBFC spokesperson Sue Clark. 'The only reason we cut films is if the distributor wants a lower category for a film than the material in the film allows or if there is something in the film which is illegal.'

Clark defends the role of the BBFC saying: 'People like a system...and want a system that tells them what to expect from a film.'

Classified

Under the law of the 1985 Cinemas Act (which this year is being updated with the Licensing Act), it is a requirement that all films carry a classification. And although it is still the responsibility of local authorities, they choose, on the whole, to accept the decisions of the BBFC.

But there have been times when the BBFC has been overruled. In June 2002 *Spider-Man* was downgraded by a very small number of local authorities which had come under pressure from cinemas and parents to lower the BBFC's 12A rating of the film.

(The BBFC had found the levels of violence in *Spider-Man* to make the film a borderline '15' rating and not suitable for a 'PG' classification.)

Video and children

Information from the Video Standards Council

When your child asks to watch a video or DVD there are probably three questions that you should ask yourself.

- How old is your child?
- What do they want to watch?
- Is it suitable?

The last question is probably the most important as, who knows your child better than you do? In the end it is your responsibility to make sure that your child doesn't watch anything unsuitable.

Even when you do decide what your child should watch it's very often difficult to control what your child actually watches, sometimes without your knowing. It's easy enough to leave a video or DVD, which is suitable for you to watch, by the television set when you go out.

Video/DVD and games titles classified 12, 15 and 18 are considered unsuitable for children or young teenagers below the specified ages

What an opportunity! Children like nothing better than to do what they are not supposed to do, especially if they think they can get away with it. Don't make it easy for them. Would you leave an open bottle of whisky, packet of cigarettes or packet of aspirins within easy reach of a seven-year-old? Think about it.

Older brothers and sisters can be a problem in more ways than one. Young teenagers can be the most difficult to control. They are young adults in the making and want to do adult things. This is fine and there are videos and DVDs which are perfectly suitable for them to see, but, not when their five-year-old sister or

brother is in the room.

And, what are your children watching at their friends' houses? Sometimes they'll tell you and sometimes they don't. If they don't then perhaps you should find out. The fact that some parents are irresponsible doesn't mean that you should be.

In the end it's up to you.

The classifications

With certain exceptions all video/DVD titles (and some games) have, by law, to be classified by the British Board of Film Classification (BBFC) before they can be made available to the public.

The BBFC is the body appointed by Government to fulfil this task. It is a serious criminal offence to supply a video/DVD/game which should have been classified and which has not been.

The exceptions for video/DVD are titles which are designed to be informative, educational or instructive or are concerned with sport, religion or music. Video and computer games are also generally exempt from legal classification. The law does not require videos/DVDs that are exempt from classification to be marked as such but you'll very often see an unofficial 'E' symbol on the sleeve. For exempt video and computer games a voluntary age-rating system is used (please refer to the GAMES section of the Video Standards Council website).

Even if a video/DVD or game is apparently exempt from legal classification it can lose this exemption if it shows such things as sexual activity or gross violence. If it loses its exemption then, by law, it has to

be legally classified.

Videos/DVD (and some games) which are legally required to be classified will be classified in one or other of the following six general categories: U, Uc, PG, 12, 15 and 18.

You'll see the classifications marked on sleeves and labels.

It's important to note that videos, DVDs and games classified PG as well as those classified Uc and U may be legally supplied to children and other people of all ages. The 12, 15 and 18 classifications restrict supply to people of and above the specified age. It is a serious criminal offence for a shop owner to supply a video, DVD or game with an age-restricted classification to someone below the specified age.

Classifications are given to enable you to make an informed choice as to what you allow your child to watch. Video/DVD and games titles classified 12, 15 and 18 are considered unsuitable for children or young teenagers below the specified ages. You may, on occasions, disagree with a classification that has been given but, if you do, then the responsibility is yours.

In the end it is up to you.

- The above information is reprinted with kind permission from the Video Standards Council. Visit www.videostandards.org.uk for more information.

Remote, no control

The parents who don't know what their children are watching on TV

One parent in four has no idea what their children watched on television last night, it has emerged.

As the pressure on both parents to go out to work intensifies, many are leaving youngsters unsupervised in front of the TV for long periods.

Some fear, however, that they are being exposed to violent or sexually explicit programmes.

A survey found that more than a third feel guilty about their inability to monitor what their children are watching.

And a similar proportion admit that they do not trust their youngsters to restrict themselves to programmes suitable for their age.

For the survey, research company TNS interviewed 356 families across the country. It found that two-thirds of children aged between two and 12 watch TV without supervision

Although half of the parents questioned said they regarded TV as a positive influence on their children, the same number had deep misgivings about programmes containing sex, violence and swearing.

For the survey, research company TNS interviewed 356 families across the country.

It found that two-thirds of children aged between two and 12 watch TV without supervision.

The findings will fuel concern about the content of the programmes that pre-teens are watching and the impact this is having on their development. Previous research has shown that children who have sets in their rooms do less well at school.

By Matt Born
Media Editor

In response to parents' fears, a range of devices are due to come on the market which will allow them to restrict what their children watch.

In the autumn Sky is to start selling a system which will enable parents to block channels so that they can be viewed only by using a secret code number.

It will also give them the option of setting their own 8pm watershed on any channel. This means they can bar anyone from viewing the channel after that time. Last week, Ed Richards, senior partner at the media regulator Ofcom, told a conference of TV executives that the growth of digital technology threatened to render the 9pm watershed redundant.

'How do we think about the watershed when the ten-year-old is watching a PVR (personal video recorder)-stored 18-rated movie in the morning while the parents are out doing the shopping?' he asked the Westminster Media Forum. Children's charities yesterday

welcomed the introduction of better controls. Phillip Noyes, director of public policy at the NSPCC, said: 'Parents need to monitor that their young children are watching appropriate TV programmes and other broadcast material.'

■ This article first appeared in the *Daily Mail*, 25 July 2005.

- NOW THAT WE'RE ALONE...

Bullying and screen violence

Puttnam blames violent films for increase in playground bullying

By Sarah Womack

Lord Puttnam, the Oscar-winning producer, blamed Hollywood films for fuelling a culture of bullying in British schools.

The Labour peer said films that featured violence and aggression 'devoid of human consequences' were leading to the growth of bullying in the playground, with children imitating what they saw on the big and small screens.

'For too long the movies have been playing games with reality, playing with it in such a way as to allow actions to become entirely divorced from their consequences'

He added that films were dumbing down and failing to address real moral problems.

'For too long the movies have been playing games with reality, playing with it in such a way as to allow actions to become entirely divorced from their consequences,' he told a conference in London organised by the Anti-Bullying Alliance.

'Sensation has come to eclipse almost everything – bigger and better explosions that miraculously don't kill the most important of protagonists; simulated plane crashes in which the right people somehow survive; and most common of all, shootings which manage to create victims without widows or orphans.'

Lord Puttnam, who produced *The Killing Fields*, *Midnight Express* and *Chariots of Fire*, said films often ignored the consequences of actions.

'In how many movies do we see a policeman walk up a garden path to tell a woman that her husband has been killed? And then perhaps witness her having to decide whether to tell her 12-year-old child, who is just about to appear in the school play, that her father is dead? Should she tell her now or wait until bedtime?

'This is the stuff of real human drama. This is the all too frequent consequence of tragic actions. Yet with some recent, notable exceptions, here is a whole world of human experience which has been effectively abandoned to the simplicities of the small screen.'

His comments follow the death of 12-year-old Nathan Jones, a pupil at King's Wood school in Harold Hill, Essex. He was found hanged at his home in Romford, and Havering council is investigating claims that he was being bullied.

Lord Puttnam, the UK president of Unicef and a former chairman of the General Teaching Council, said the media should be a 'force for good in promoting the overwhelming value of social coherence'.

Speaking after the conference, he was particularly critical of films such as *Gangster No 1*, *Falling Down*, *Man on Fire* and *Natural Born Killers*.

He admitted that the media was not 'wholly to blame' for the rise in bullying, and fell short of calling for tighter censorship. But he urged film makers to 'think far more deeply about the impact of their work'.

20 April 2005

Film classification

Information on age ratings from the British Board of Film Classification

Universal classification

It is impossible to predict what might upset any particular child. But a 'U' film should be suitable for audiences aged four years and over. U films should be set within a positive moral framework and should offer reassuring counterbalances to any violence, threat or horror.

Videos classified 'Uc' are particularly suitable for pre-school children and normally raise none of the issues set out below.

Theme
Treatment of problematic themes must be sensitive and appropriate for a younger audience.

Language
Infrequent use only of very mild bad language.

Nudity
Occasional natural nudity, with no sexual context.

Sex
Mild sexual behaviour (e.g. kissing) and references only (e.g. to 'making love').

Violence
Mild violence only. Occasional mild threat or menace only.

Imitable techniques
No emphasis on realistic or easily accessible weapons. No potentially dangerous behaviour which young children are likely to copy.

Horror
Horror effects should be mild and brief and should take account of the presence of very young viewers. The outcome should be reassuring.

Drugs
No references to illegal drugs or drug misuse unless there is a clear educational purpose or clear anti-drug message suitable for the audience.

'PG' Parental Guidance

'PG' Parental Guidance – General viewing, but some scenes may be unsuitable for young children.

Unaccompanied children of any age may watch. A 'PG' film should not disturb a child aged around eight or older. However, parents are advised to consider whether the content may upset younger or more sensitive children.

Theme
Where more serious issues are featured (e.g. domestic violence, racist abuse) nothing in their treatment should condone the behaviour.

Language
Mild bad language only.

Nudity
Natural nudity, with no sexual context.

Sex
Sexual activity may be implied, but should be discreet and infrequent. Mild sex references and innuendo only.

Violence
Moderate violence, without detail, may be allowed, if justified by its setting (e.g. historic, comedy or fantasy).

Imitable techniques
No glamorisation of realistic or easily accessible weapons. No detail of potentially dangerous behaviour which young children are likely to copy.

Horror
Frightening sequences should not be prolonged or intense. Fantasy settings may be a mitigating factor.

Drugs
Any references to illegal drugs or drug misuse must be innocuous or carry a suitable anti-drug message.

12A / 12

12A – Suitable for 12 years and over. Noone younger than 12 may see a '12A' film in a cinema unless accompanied by an adult. Noone younger than 12 may rent or buy a '12'-rated video or DVD. Responsibility for allowing under-12s to view lies with the accompanying or supervising adult.

Theme
Mature themes are acceptable, but their treatment must be suitable for young teenagers.

Language
The use of strong language (e.g. 'fuck') must be infrequent. Racist abuse is also of particular concern.

Nudity
Nudity is allowed, but in a sexual context must be brief and discreet.

Sex
Sexual activity may be implied. Sex references may reflect what is likely to be familiar to most adolescents but should not go beyond what is suitable for them.

Violence
Violence must not dwell on detail. There should be no emphasis on injuries or blood. Sexual violence may only be implied or briefly and discreetly indicated.

Imitable techniques
Dangerous techniques (e.g. combat, hanging, suicide and self-harming) should not dwell on imitable detail or appear pain or harm-free. Easily accessible weapons should not be glamorised.

Horror
Sustained moderate threat and menace are permitted. Occasional gory moments only.

Drugs
Any misuse of drugs must be infrequent and should not be glamorised or instructional.

15

'15' – Suitable only for 15 years and over.

Noone younger than 15 may see a '15' film in a cinema. Noone younger than 15 may rent or buy a '15'-rated video or DVD.

Theme
No theme is prohibited, provided the treatment is appropriate to 15-year-olds.

Language
There may be frequent use of strong language (e.g. 'fuck'). But the

strongest terms (e.g. 'cunt') will be acceptable only where justified by the context. Continued aggressive use of the strongest language is unlikely to be acceptable.

Nudity

Nudity may be allowed in a sexual context but without strong detail. There are no constraints on nudity in a non-sexual or educational context.

Sex

Sexual activity may be portrayed but without strong detail. There may be strong verbal references to sexual behaviour.

Violence

Violence may be strong but may not dwell on the infliction of pain or injury. Scenes of sexual violence must be discreet and brief.

Imitable techniques

Dangerous techniques (e.g. combat, hanging, suicide and self-harming) should not dwell on imitable detail. Easily accessible weapons should not be glamorised.

Horror

Strong threat and menace are permitted. The strongest gory images are unlikely to be acceptable.

Drugs

Drug taking may be shown but the film as a whole must not promote or encourage drug misuse.

18

'18' – Suitable only for adults

Noone younger than 18 may see an '18' film in a cinema. Noone younger than 18 may rent or buy an '18'-rated video.

In line with the consistent findings of the BBFC's public consultations, at '18' the BBFC's guideline concerns will not normally override the wish that adults should be free to chose their own entertainment, within the law. Exceptions are most likely in the following areas:

- where material or treatment appears to the Board to risk harm to individuals or, through their behaviour, to society – e.g. any detailed portrayal of violent or dangerous acts, or of illegal drug use, which is likely to promote the activity. The Board may also intervene with portrayals of sexual violence which might, e.g., eroticise or endorse sexual assault.

- the more explicit images of sexual activity – unless they can be exceptionally justified by context and the work is not a 'sex work' as defined below.

In the case of videos and DVDs, which may be more accessible to younger viewers, intervention may be more frequent. For the same reason, and because of the different way in which they are experienced, the Board may take a more precautionary approach in the case of those digital games which are covered by the Video Recordings Act.

Sex education at '18'

Where sex material genuinely seeks to inform and educate in matters such as human sexuality, safe sex and health, exceptions to the normal constraints on explicit images may be made in the public interest. Such explicit detail must be kept to the minimum necessary to illustrate the educational or instructional points being made.

Sex works at '18'

Sex works are works, normally on video or DVD, whose primary purpose is sexual arousal or stimulation. Sex works containing material which may be simulated are generally passed '18', while sex works containing clear images of real sex are confined to the 'R18' category.

R18

'R18' – To be shown only in specially licensed cinemas, or supplied only in licensed sex shops, and to adults of not less than 18 years.

The 'R18' category is a special and legally restricted classification primarily for explicit works of consenting sex between adults. Films may only be shown to adults

in specially licensed cinemas, and videos may be supplied to adults only in licensed sex shops. 'R18' videos may not be supplied by mail order.

The following content is not acceptable:

- any material which is in breach of the criminal law, including material judged to be obscene under the current interpretation of the Obscene Publications Act 1959.

- material (including dialogue) likely to encourage an interest in sexually abusive activity (e.g. paedophilia, incest, rape) which may include adults role-playing as non-adults.

- the portrayal of any sexual activity which involves lack of consent (whether real or simulated). Any form of physical restraint which prevents participants from indicating a withdrawal of consent.

- the infliction of pain or physical harm, real or (in a sexual context) simulated. Some allowance may be made for mild consensual activity. Penetration by any object likely to cause actual harm or associated with violence.

- any sexual threats, humiliation or abuse which does not form part of a clearly consenting role-playing game. Strong abuse, even if consensual, is unlikely to be acceptable.

These guidelines will be applied to the same standard whether the activity is heterosexual or homosexual.

- Information from the British Board of Film Classification. Visit www.bbfc.co.uk for more.

© BBFC

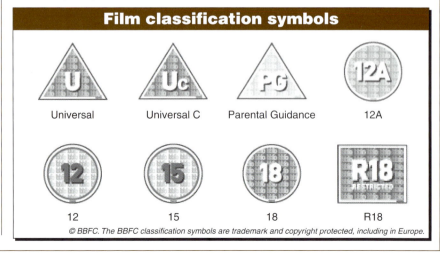

Film classification symbols

Universal — Universal C — Parental Guidance — 12A

12 — 15 — 18 — R18

The letter of the law

The Video Recordings Act 1984

The Act essentially did two things:

With certain exceptions it made it illegal to sell or rent a video (this includes a DVD) unless it had been given a legal classification (Uc, U, PG, 12, 15, or 18) by a Government-appointed body (the British Board of Film Classification).

For videos given an age-restricted classification it made it illegal to sell or rent such videos to anyone below the specified age.

The penalty for selling or renting an age-restricted video (12, 15 or 18) to someone below the specified age is a fine of up to £5,000 and/or up to 6 months in jail

The penalty for selling or renting a video which should have been classified but has not been is an unlimited fine and/or up to two years in jail. The penalty for selling or renting an age-restricted video (12, 15 or 18) to someone below the specified age is a fine of up to £5,000 and/or up to 6 months in jail.

The Criminal Justice Act 1988

Extended the powers of enforcing the 1984 Act to trading standards officers.

The Criminal Justice & Public Order Act 1994

Required the BBFC to have special regard to the treatment of, inter alia, 'criminal behaviour, illegal drugs, violent behaviour or incidents, horrific behaviour or human sexual activity' in the videos that it is considering for legal classification.

The BBFC may decline to grant a classification in which case the video becomes an illegal video and cannot be legally supplied to the public.

- Video is the most regulated home entertainment medium in the UK.
- Video is more closely regulated in the UK than anywhere else in Europe.
- Video in the UK is subject to statutory pre-censorship that is unique.

Video is pre-censored under the law. Newspapers, magazines, the theatre, television, radio – even the cinema – are not. The cinema is pre-censored voluntarily. All the others are subject to voluntary controls and sanctions – mostly minor sanctions – which are retrospective.

- The above information is re-printed with kind permission from the Video Standards Council. Visit www.videostandards.org.uk for more information.

© VSC

Time spent watching television

Average time spent viewing television, video and DVD,[1] by region and sex, 2000.

Region	Male	Female
North East	208	187
North West	188	168
Yorkshire/Humber	188	170
East Midlands	167	163
West Midlands	184	162
East	161	155
London	158	151
South East	163	149
South West	169	157
Wales	190	166
Scotland	192	170
Northern Ireland	157	146
United Kingdom	175	161

minutes per day

1. Combined main and secondary activity time

Source: UK 2000 Time Use Survey, ONS. Crown copyright

Children and video games

Information from the Video Standards Council

It is probably true that most parents of children and young teenagers have grown up in the video age and therefore have a reasonable understanding of the legal classification system and an ability to decide whether a particular video/DVD is suitable for their children. If all else fails a parent can always watch the video/DVD before making a decision.

This is not always the case when it comes to video and computer games where all too often the child is more adept at using the computer or games console and the parent sometimes doesn't know how to access what their child is playing. As a result it is important that parents have something to guide them when making a decision on whether a game is suitable for their children.

All too often the child is more adept at using the computer or games console and the parent sometimes doesn't know how to access what their child is playing

There are two systems for games that parents can rely upon – a legal system and a voluntary system.

Under the law games are generally exempt from the legal classification system that applies to video/DVD. However, this exemption can be lost usually because the game shows realistic scenes of gross violence or sexual activity. If this happens the game must be legally classified and will receive one or other of the classification certificates described in the VIDEO section of the Video Standards Council website. Usually the game will receive an age-restricted classification (12, 15

or 18) which makes it illegal for a shopkeeper to supply the game to anyone below the specified age.

Accordingly parents have the comfort of knowing that games of a more extreme nature are dealt with by the law. There is nothing wrong with a game with an age-restricted classification. It simply means that the game is not suitable for young children and is suitable for a more mature audience.

Since 1993 about 5% of games have lost their general exemption and have been given legal classifications.

This leaves about 95% of games which are not covered by the law. In 1993 the VSC joined forces with the Entertainment & Leisure Software Publishers' Association (ELSPA) which is the trade body representing the large majority of games publishers in the UK.

It was recognised that whilst the large majority of games were and would probably remain exempt from legal classification this did not mean that all exempt games were suitable for children of all ages. As a result of consultation between the VSC, ELSPA and a number of outside bodies (including

Video game age ratings symbols

The ELSPA voluntary age-suitability rating symbols

The PEGI age-suitability rating symbols

The PEGI content descriptor symbols

VIOLENCE   DRUGS   FEAR   DISCRIMINATION   SEX/NUDITY   BAD LANGUAGE

© Video Standards Council

organisations concerned with family and child welfare) the voluntary system of age-rating for games exempt from legal classification was devised. The system belongs to ELSPA and was administered by the VSC as an independent third party not influenced by commercial considerations.

Under the voluntary system games are rated at one of four different levels – ages 3+, 11+, 15+ and 18+.

These voluntary age-suitability ratings enable parents to make an informed choice when buying a game for their children.

It should be noted that the ratings relate to the content of the game and not to how difficult the game is to play. A chess game would probably be a 3+ but would hardly be recommended for toddlers.

Since 1994 until the Spring of 2003 over 6,000 games were rated under the ELSPA voluntary system with 67% receiving a 3+, 22% an 11+, 10% a 15+ and less than 1% an 18+. It was always unlikely that many games would receive an 18+ under the voluntary system as any game reaching this level would probably have already lost its exemption and have to be legally classified.

These figures dispel the myth that most games are of a violent nature. The truth is quite the reverse.

In the Spring of 2003 the ELSPA system was superseded by a new pan-European system operating in more than 20 countries across Europe.

The PEGI system belongs to the Interactive Software Federation of Europe (ISFE) which is based in Belgium. ISFE have contracted the administration of the system to the Netherlands Institute for the Classification of Audiovisual Media (NICAM) which is based in Holland. The VSC acts as NICAM's agent in the UK.

Under this new system games are rated at one of five different age-levels:

The 12+ and 16+ are generally equivalent to the 11+ and 15+ given under the ELSPA system. The changes were made to accommodate differing views held in the participating countries.

The 7+ rating is a new age-rating level not used under the ELSPA system and will be used for games that do not contain anything generally unsuitable but which may nevertheless be frightening or scary to very young children (e.g. creaking doors in a haunted house, rustling in the undergrowth).

A feature of the PEGI system is the use of content descriptors as well as age-ratings on the packaging for games. The content descriptors will indicate the main reason/s why a game is given a particular age-rating. This additional information should provide more help to parents.

For more information about the PEGI system or games generally visit the pegi.info or askaboutgames.com websites which can be accessed from the LINKS page of the VSC website. An askaboutgames leaflet designed to inform parents about age ratings for games can be obtained from the DOWNLOADS page of the VSC site.

■ Information from the Video Standards Council. Visit www.videostandards.org for more.

© VSC

Violence and video games

How video games are training the brain for violence

Playing violent video games 'trains' the mind to react aggressively in real-life situations, research suggests.

For the first time, scientists have worked out what goes on in the brain when a violent game is being played, discovering in the process that players treat the situation as if it was real.

The emotional centres of the brain, which guide acceptable behaviour, shut down and cognitive or rational areas take over when a threat emerges.

This leads players to prepare to react violently and unemotionally to the threat.

Scientists say those who play such games regularly are conditioning their brains to respond the same way in real life.

Dr Klaus Mathiak, of the University of Aachen in Germany, recruited 13 men aged 18 to 26 who played video games for an average of two hours every day for the study.

He asked them to play a violent game – during which they had to kill terrorists and rescue hostages – while having their brains scannned.

As violence became imminent areas of the brain associated with emotions and appropriate social responses were suppressed. He concluded that violent games 'train the brain to react with this pattern'.

The research, published in the magazine *New Scientist*, reinforces fears that playing violent computer games can lead to copycat behaviour in real life, particularly among youngsters.

It follows last year's outcry over the ultra-violent game Manhunt, which was implicated in the murder of a teenage boy.

The parents of Stefan Pakeerah called for it to be banned after the 14-year-old died at the hands of Warren Leblanc, 17, who was said to be obsessed with the game.

Professor Mark Griffiths, head of psychology at Nottingham Trent University, warned that children were more at risk of being affected by violent video games than adults as their brains were not yet fully formed.

'Society as a whole has become more desensitised to violence because of the increase in violent images in films, on television and in computer games,' he added.

■ This article first appeared in the *Daily Mail*, 23 June 2005.

Violence in the media

Birmingham researchers call for a public health approach to violence in the media

Researchers at the University of Birmingham's Centre for Forensic and Family Psychology are calling for a public health approach to media violence and have published guidelines to reduce the effects of violent imagery on children and adolescents in an article in today's issue of *The Lancet*.

The availability of video film, satellite and cable TV in the home means that children now have access to violent media inappropriate to their age, developmental stage and mental health. In recent years, the proliferation of the Internet as well as interactive video and computer games containing violence has limited the effectiveness of parental control.

Studies have proved that violence in the media has short-term influences on thoughts and emotions, and increases the likelihood of aggressive behaviours in children and adolescents

Research has found that the influence of media violence on children's behaviour is as strong as the influence that the use of condoms has on the prevention of the spread of the HIV virus or the effect that passive smoking at work has on lung cancer.

Studies have proved that violence in the media has short-term influences on thoughts and emotions, and increases the likelihood of aggressive behaviours in children and adolescents, especially in boys. Some studies on the effects of media violence on children and young people have emphasised fear as an outcome.

UNIVERSITY OF BIRMINGHAM

This association is especially relevant to news programmes depicting disasters such as the terrorist attacks on the World Trade Centre in 2001.

Professor Kevin Browne, Director of the Centre for Forensic and Family Psychology and lead researcher, says, 'Controls over age restriction are more difficult to implement in the home than in the cinema, for example. We are asking that parents show greater responsibility for their children's viewing habits by recommending that parents and caregivers exercise the same care with violent media entertainment aimed at adults as they do with medication and chemicals around the home. Carelessness with material containing extreme violence and sexual imagery might even be considered a form of emotional child maltreatment.

'There is evidence to suggest that violence in the media has become more acceptable to policy makers and the public over time with more explicit violent imagery than ever before, but research does not support the view that film makers will lose revenue by reducing violent imagery. Producers need to recognise the potential impact of violence on vulnerable audiences who may not have the capacity or the will to see the violence in the context of the story.

'Parents need to take an educational rather than censorial approach to viewing age-appropriate violent material with children and helping them to critically appraise what they see in terms of its realism, justification and consequences.'
18 February 2005

■ The above information is reprinted with kind permission from the University of Birmingham. Visit www.birmingham.ac.uk for more information.
© University of Birmingham 2006

Children and screen violence

Screen violence 'can harm even well-behaved children'

Graphic violence on television and in computer games can have a harmful effect on children who were previously well-behaved, a study has revealed.

The research showed that teenagers with no previous history of aggression could potentially suffer from loss of control and poor decision-making after being exposed to violent images.

The study found that the part of the brain which controls these functions was impaired by what they saw.

The findings have confirmed the fears of child campaigners who have called for them to be protected from screen violence.

> *Teenagers with no previous history of aggression could potentially suffer from loss of control and poor decision-making after being exposed to violent images*

Dr Michelle Elliott, of children's charity Kidscape, said: 'This will strike a chord with every parent. You can't feed children a diet of violence without an effect. The video game industry keeps saying there isn't but you can't think that bad things don't influence children. I hope they take notice of this.'

The research follows last year's outcry over the ultra-violent game Manhunt, which was implicated in the savage murder of a teenage boy.

The parents of Stefan Pakeerah called for it to be banned after the 14-year-old suffered a horrific death at the hands of 17-year-old Warren Leblanc, said to be obsessed with the game.

Previous research has found that youngsters already predisposed to violence are encouraged to carry out attacks and commit other crimes such as joyriding. As part of the new research – at the Indiana University School of Medicine and published in the *Journal of Computer Assisted Tomography* – scientists looked at two groups each consisting of 14 adolescent boys and five girls.

All the members of one group had a history of violence and had been diagnosed with disruptive behaviour disorder (DBD). Members of the second group had no past record of behavioural problems.

The volunteers were asked to take part in a concentration test after being exposed to varying amounts of violent media in their everyday lives.

Brain scans showed that all members of the DBD group displayed a reduced amount of brain activity in the frontal cortex – responsible for decision-making and self-control – whatever their exposure to violent images. Among the second group, normal frontal brain activity was seen in those spared heavy doses of violence in the media.

But those who were highly exposed suffered the same effects as their disruptive peers.

Study leader Professor Vincent Matthews said: 'We found that individuals in the normal group with high media violence exposure showed a brain activation pattern similar to the pattern of the aggressive group.'

Co-researcher Dr William Kronenberger warned that more work was needed before firm conclusions could be drawn.

But he said any association found to exist between exposure to violent images and brain functioning should be taken seriously.

■ This article was first published in the *Daily Mail*, 13 June 2005.
© 2005 Associated Newspapers Ltd

Are we too frightened of fear?

Scary films probably don't harm our children, if viewed in the right way, says Deborah Holder

Bad news for younger fans of *Star Wars*. According to producer George Lucas, the latest and last instalment, *Revenge of the Sith*, is 'way too dark' for five- or six-year-olds. They could still see the film accompanied by an adult, as British censors have given the film a 12A rating, but Lucas advises against it.

> *There has been relatively little research into the role of fear in child development, due largely to the ethical problems of terrifying small children in the interests of science*

Should parents take heed? Will their small children be traumatised by Darth Vader, or does a little bit of what scares them actually do young children some good? It's a tough call, and one that many parents have recently had to make in their own sitting rooms, thanks to the new series of *Doctor Who*. A recent episode featuring stalking corpses drew almost 100 complaints. The BBC initially said that the series, broadcast at 7pm, should only be watched by the over-eights but now they have 'left it to parents' discretion to ultimately decide'.

There has been relatively little research into the role of fear in child development, due largely to the ethical problems of terrifying small children in the interests of science. 'We're not allowed, for instance, to use the sort of imagery the BBC can

on *Dr Who*,' says Dr Andy Field, a senior lecturer in psychology at Sussex University whose research has focused on fear in children and the development of phobias. 'But, in my view, fear is a normal part of growing up.'

General fearfulness in children, he says, decreases as age increases, stabilising at around 14. 'In infancy, children tend to fear stimuli in their immediate environment such as loud noises or separation from a parent, but as a child matures, these fears shift to incorporate anticipatory events and more abstract fears.'

In terms of television, fears follow a similar pattern. 'Children under about five are totally driven by what they see and hear,' say Dr Brian Young, author of many national reports on children and television

imagery. 'They are creatures of the senses and will be scared of something only for as long as they can see it. Older children build up expectations about what "might" happen.'

Thankfully, exposure to mildly frightening information and imagery tends not to have long-term effects, says Dr Field. 'In our experiments, the children may change their thoughts and behaviours short-term, but do not develop pervasive fears as long as they are debriefed at the end of the experiment.'

In a sense, 'debriefing' is something which happens quite naturally in many homes. 'We will often discuss programmes after they have finished,' says Rebecca, a 42-year-old mother of two, 'especially if I think the children have been confused or frightened by what they've seen.'

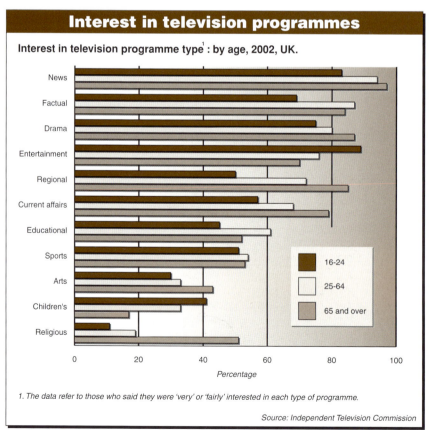

Interest in television programmes

Interest in television programme type[1] : by age, 2002, UK.

1. The data refer to those who said they were 'very' or 'fairly' interested in each type of programme.

Source: Independent Television Commission

If things do become too scary, however, the consequences may be more serious and could lead a child to develop a phobia. 'Individual temperament is a factor,' says Dr Field, 'so you could say that it's best left to the parents' discretion as they will know if they have an anxious child. Watching in the safe environment of your family is a good idea and, if something scary crops up, then it's probably better to keep

---

'One striking thing we found with our research was that it's harder for parents to know how to deal with factual material like war, crime and disasters, which children often find more disturbing than fiction'

---

watching and let your fear subside, rather than to stop watching – which simply reinforces your fear. The most sensible thing to do is to video it, watch it yourself and, if you think the imagery is too scary, then not to let them see it at all, as opposed to turning off the television when your children already have a disturbing image in their heads.'

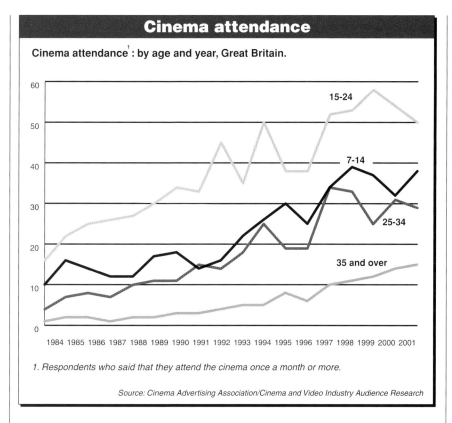

Cinema attendance

Cinema attendance[1]: by age and year, Great Britain.

1. Respondents who said that they attend the cinema once a month or more.

Source: Cinema Advertising Association/Cinema and Video Industry Audience Research

It could be argued, of course, that the controversy surrounding *Dr Who* is a distraction from a much bigger problem – the daily news bulletins, which ride roughshod over watersheds with their often horrific accounts of murder and violent crime.

Professor Buckingham agrees that news can be an issue. 'One striking thing we found with our research was that it's harder for parents to know how to deal with factual material like war, crime and disasters, which children often find more disturbing than fiction. In the case of a film, parents said they could talk about it afterwards, remind kids that it was made up, explain the special effects and generally demystify it. But with factual material such as murders or high profile child abductions, what can you say? – "Things like that don't happen often, but they do happen."'

Perhaps cowering behind the sofa is not such a bad compromise after all.

18 May 2005

© *Telegraph Group Limited 2006*

The soaps full of filth

Swearing goes up before the watershed

By Matt Born
Media Editor

Soap operas and reality shows are responsible for a sharp increase in swearing on television before the 9pm watershed, a survey has found.

Viewers reported a general coarsening of standards across the main channels, with much more explicit swearing and sexual imagery.

Big Brother, *Trisha*, *The Osbournes* and *Hell's Kitchen* with Gordon Ramsay were highlighted as examples of programmes that inflict strong language on viewers.

The BBC1 soap *EastEnders* was also mentioned – although those interviewed for the survey were unable to recall specific examples – as were music channels such as MTV that feature 'gangsta rap'.

The survey, carried out by media regulator Ofcom, found Channel 4 and, to a lesser extent, Five, were leading the way in increasing profanity.

> 'Nearly everyone in the research thought that there was more sexual imagery on television than before, that it was more explicit and started earlier in the evening,' Ofcom said in its survey report

Offensive language on soaps and reality shows was particularly disliked 'due to the early transmission time and large family viewing'.

One of those questioned said: 'On *EastEnders* about three or fours years ago they weren't even allowing the terms "bitch", "slag" or "cow" . . . whereas now it is coming out.'

Another said: 'It has got worse, especially on reality shows, for example, *Big Brother*.'

Although bad language topped viewers' list of concerns, they were also worried about the increase in sexual imagery.

'Nearly everyone in the research thought that there was more sexual imagery on television than before, that it was more explicit and started earlier in the evening,' Ofcom said in its survey report.

'Parents in particular tended to worry about [it], largely because they felt it could lead to premature sexualisation of their children.'

Broadcasters have been criticised recently for 'eroding' the watershed by showing adult-orientated content before or shortly after 9pm.

In its report, *Language and Sexual Imagery in Broadcasting: A Contextual Investigation*, Ofcom said there was widespread support for retaining the watershed.

Indeed, many of those questioned said they would like it reinforced and extended beyond 9pm – particularly at weekends when children are more

likely to stay up late.

Parents were especially keen for sexual content to be restricted to outside 'family viewing hours' – by which they meant after 10pm.

BBC2 drew flak recently over its drama *Rome* which featured explicit sex and full-frontal nudity at 9.10pm. The Ofcom report, which was based on interviews with 173 viewers, found they had different expectations of channels and programmes.

While BBC1 should be the 'gold standard' in terms of maintaining

standards, they felt Channel 4 and Five could be allowed more leeway in terms of risqué material.

Similarly, swearing on programmes such as *The Osbournes* – a docu-soap about the domestic life of the heavy metal singer Ozzy Osbourne – was seen as more acceptable because 'it's funny' and 'you expect it'.

Those surveyed felt broadcasters had a responsibility to uphold standards. And they accused programme makers of cynically trying to shock audiences in order to chase ratings

---

Those questioned conceded swearing and sexual imagery was more widespread in all areas of society – and that to some extent television was merely reflecting that.

At the same time, they felt broadcasters had a responsibility to uphold standards. And they accused programme makers of cynically trying to shock audiences in order to chase ratings,

'It's not young people who are making these programmes – it's older people who are making them for exploitative reasons,' said one parent.

A handful of viewers interviewed said they thought language on television had improved.

The culprits

Big Brother
The original pretence of a 'social experiment' has long since been jettisoned by Channel 4 in favour of shock tactics including fights, swearing and as much nudity as possible.

The reality TV show has repeatedly fallen foul of the regulators. The latest series also featured racism and explicit sex. Despite being shown at 10pm, it still drew a sackful of complaints.

Trisha
The Channel Five daytime talkshow hosted by Trisha Goddard is known for its unsavoury subject matter. Three years ago the 47-year-old presenter was criticised by TV watchdogs after featuring 'love-rat' specials straight after children's programmes.

Trisha Exposes Britain's Biggest Love Rats showed results of paternity tests live on air, with the audience chanting 'Who's the daddy?' It received 38 complaints.

EastEnders
The BBC1 soap has been heavily criticised for the infiltration of 'thugs' into its storylines. 'Bitch', 'slapper' and 'tart' are all part of the Walford vernacular while a perceived increase in on-screen violence has also prompted complaints.

Hell's Kitchen
Putting Gordon Ramsay in a kitchen full of celebrities was always likely to prove an explosive recipe. The chef's industrial language drew a flurry of complaints from viewers – even though it was broadcast post-watershed at 9pm and carried an on-screen warning. ITV was duly censured for Ramsay's language.

They pointed out the demise of the racist remarks commonplace in the 1960s and 70s on shows such as *Love Thy Neighbour*.

But in its conclusions, Ofcom said most 'believed that offensive language had increased over time and that the language used has become stronger'.

'Respondents felt swearing and offensive language occurred across a range of programming types and channels; that it started earlier in the evening; and that soaps and reality programmes had contributed to this decline more than other genres.'

■ This article was first published in the *Daily Mail*, 22 November 2005.
© 2005 Associated Newspapers Ltd

- Media don't exist just to entertain us. In a democracy the media provide us with important information. They can give us a range of opinions which we might not otherwise hear. (page 1)

- A free press is allowed (within reason) to print and say what it likes about the government. Sometimes the government decides to restrict information during an emergency, such as a war. (page 2)

- In the UK, a handful of companies own most of the media. The biggest company is the News Corporation. (page 5)

- Media companies tend to support one particular political viewpoint. This can have a huge influence on how people vote. (page 5)

- Among YouGov survey respondents, the BBC was named as the most trusted news brand in the UK. (page 6)

- Amidst the growing recognition of the importance of press freedom for democracy and development, in 1993 the United Nations General Assembly proclaimed that May 3 is 'World Press Freedom Day'. (page 6)

- Blasphemy is not a statutory offence. The Blasphemy Act was repealed in 1969. It remains a common law offence. (page 16)

- 41% of those surveyed by MORI felt it was justifiable for a Danish newspaper to publish cartoons of the prophet Muhammed, even knowing they would cause offence. 42% felt it was not justified. (page 17)

- Political parties and the government have special media and publicity departments that deal with their public image and decide what news should be released and when. (page 17)

- 75% who took part in an online poll by AOL felt freedom of speech was a right. 25% felt that it was sometimes wrong. (page 18)

- Current technology makes it effectively impossible to censor the written word, theatre censorship was abolished in 1968, and there has never been any systematic regulation of other art forms – anyone seeking to clamp down on such events must mount a private prosecution, a lengthy and expensive process. (page 22)

- The British Board of Film Censors (BBFC), an independent non-profit-making body (funded by fees), was established by the film industry in 1912 to bring consistency to classification. (page 23)

- To ensure its guidelines represent the majority view of the public towards themes of sex, bad language, drugs and violence, the BBFC undertakes regular public consultations. (page 24)

- Though it might seem to the contrary, arguments with film distributors over cuts and classification are apparently extremely rare. (page 25)

- A survey found that more than a third of parents feel guilty about their inability to monitor what their children are watching. And a similar proportion admit that they do not trust their youngsters to restrict themselves to programmes suitable for their age. (page 27)

- A 'U' film should be suitable for audiences aged four years and over. U films should be set within a positive moral framework and should offer reassuring counterbalances to any violence, threat or horror. (page 29)

- Males in the UK spend an average of 175 minutes per day watching television, video and DVD. Females spend an average of 161 minutes per day on these activities. (page 31)

- Under the law games are generally exempt from the legal classification system that applies to video/DVD. However, this exemption can be lost usually because the game shows realistic scenes of gross violence or sexual activity. (page 32)

- Playing violent video games 'trains' the mind to react aggressively in real-life situations, research suggests. (page 33)

- Research has found that the influence of media violence on children's behaviour is as strong as the influence that the use of condoms has on the prevention of the spread of the HIV virus or the effect that passive smoking at work has on lung cancer. (page 34)

- Graphic violence on television and in computer games can have a harmful effect on children who were previously well-behaved, a study has revealed. (page 35)

- There has been relatively little research into the role of fear in child development, due largely to the ethical problems of terrifying small children in the interests of science. (page 36)

- Soap operas and reality shows are responsible for a sharp increase in swearing on television before the 9pm watershed, a survey has found. (page 38)

GLOSSARY

Blasphemy
Defined by law as involving 'any contemptuous, reviling, scurrilous or ludicrous matter relating to God, Jesus Christ, the Bible or the formularies of the Church of England as by law established'. In the UK, blasphemy is a common-law offence, but relates only to the Church of England.

The British Board of Film Classification (BBFC)
A body appointed by the government to classify all video and DVD releases.

Censorship
When there are restrictions on what people can see or hear, this is called censorship. By censoring something, you are preventing the whole truth coming out or stopping something being heard or seen at all.

Classifications
Also called age ratings. Films on DVD/video and computer games must carry a classification indicating a minimum age at which the material should be watched or played. It is a criminal offence for a retailer to supply an age-restricted video or game to someone below the required age.

Freedom of expression
Also called freedom of speech, free speech. This is protected by Article 19 of the Universal Declaration of Human Rights, which states that: 'Everyone has the right to freedom of opinion and expression; this right includes freedom to hold opinions without interference and to seek, receive and impart information and ideas through any media and regardless of frontiers'.

Free press
A free press is one which is not censored or controlled by a government. It allows us to find out what we want to know without restrictions.

The Freedom of Information Act
The Freedom of Information Act states that there should be free access to information about the government, individuals and businesses.

Non-violent direct action (NVDA)
Peaceful protesting. This means that you can take part in public protest but that it does not involve violence against property or persons.

The Video Recordings Act 1984
This act made it illegal to sell or rent a video which had not been classified, as well as making it an offence for a video retailer to supply an age-restricted product to someone under-age.

The watershed
The watershed is the name for the 9pm cut-off point in television scheduling, after which television channels can show programmes containing material which may not have been suitable for a younger audience, such as sex scenes or bad language.

ACKNOWLEDGEMENTS

The publisher is grateful for permission to reproduce the following material.

While every care has been taken to trace and acknowledge copyright, the publisher tenders its apology for any accidental infringement or where copyright has proved untraceable. The publisher would be pleased to come to a suitable arrangement in any such case with the rightful owner.

Chapter One: The Free Speech Debate

A free press, © Channel 4, Timeline: a history of free speech, © Guardian Newspapers Ltd 2006, Freedom of expression, © Crown copyright is reproduced with the permission of Her Majesty's Stationery Office, Media ownership and control, © Channel 4, The most trusted news brands, © YouGov, UNESCO and Press Freedom Day, © UNESCO, Grey area, © Guardian Newspapers Ltd 2006, The Danish cartoon controversy, © Campaign for Press and Broadcasting Freedom, When speech offends, © Human Rights Watch, Your right to protest, © TheSite.org, Double standards in freedom of expression, © Muslim News, The blasphemy law, © Campaign Against Censorship, The government and the media, © Channel 4, The Internet, © AOL, Internet companies 'must respect free speech', © 2006 CNET Networks, Inc., Backlash as Google shores up great firewall of China, © Guardian Newspapers Ltd 2006.

Chapter Two: Regulation and Censorship

Censorship and regulation, © The British Film Insititute, Classified material, © Channel 4, Video and children, © Video Standards Council, Remote, no control, © Associated Newspapers Ltd 2005, Bullying and screen violence, © Telegraph Group Ltd 2006, Film classification, © British Board of Film Classification, The letter of the law, © Video Standards Council, Children and video games, © Video Standards Council, Violence and video games, © 2005 Associated Newspapers Ltd, Violence in the media, © University of Birmingham 2006, Children and screen violence, © 2005 Associated Newspapers Ltd, Are we too frightened of fear?, © Telegraph Group Ltd 2006, The soaps full of filth, © 2005 Associated Newspapers Ltd.

Photographs and illustrations:

Pages 1, 21, 28, 38: Angelo Madrid; pages 9, 25, 35, 39: Don Hatcher; pages 13, 22: Bev Aisbett; pages 14, 27, 34, 37: Simon Kneebone; page 19: Pumpkin House.

Craig Donnellan
Cambridge
April, 2006